# Close-up

## WORKBOOK

## A1+

Phillip McElmuray

**NATIONAL GEOGRAPHIC**
**LEARNING**

Australia · Brazil · Mexico · Singapore · United Kingdom · United States

**Close-up A1+ Workbook**

Phillip McElmuray

Executive Editor: Sian Mavor

Editorial Manager: Claire Merchant

Commissioning Editor: Kayleigh Buller

Editor: Nick Stewart

Head of Production: Celia Jones

Content Project Manager: Melissa Beavis

Manufacturing Manager: Eyvett Davis

Compositor: Wild Apple Design Ltd

For product information and technology assistance, contact us at
**Cengage Learning Customer & Sales Support, cengage.com/contact**

For permission to use material from this text or product,
submit all requests online at **cengage.com/permissions**
Further permissions questions can be emailed to
**permissionrequest@cengage.com**

ISBN: 978-1-4080-9824-0

**National Geographic Learning**
Cheriton House, North Way, Andover, Hampshire, SP10 5BE
United Kingdom

National Geographic Learning, a Cengage Learning Company, has a mission to bring the world to the classroom and the classroom to life. With our English language programs, students learn about their world by experiencing it. Through our partnerships with National Geographic and TED Talks, they develop the language and skills they need to be successful global citizens and leaders.

Locate your local office at **international.cengage.com/region**

Visit National Geographic Learning online at **NGL.Cengage.com/ELT**
Visit our corporate website at **www.cengage.com**

**Photo Credits**
**Cover images:** (front cover) ©Filip Fuxa/Shutterstock Inc, (back cover) ©aodaodaodaod/Shutterstock Inc

**© Alamy:**
3; 4 Charles O. Cecil

**© Robert Harding:**
**Multiple pages (Learning Focus Icon)** Frank Fox/Okapia

**© Shutterstock:**
3 Ociacia; 4 Konstantin Shevtsov; 5 Monkey Business Images; 5 Blend Images; 5 Nattakit.K; 5 Juriah Mosin; 6 Monkey Business Images; 6 Rawpixel.com; 6 Alena Ozerova; 6 Alexander Mak; 6 Ben Neumann; 6 Artellia; 6 RimDream; 7 Loflo69; 8 Tr1sha; 8 Alex Bros; 10 YanLev; 11 Robert_s; 11 Wouter Tolenaars; 11 Windu; 11 Xiaorui; 11 PriceM; 11 Gogoiso; 11 Chiyacat; 11 Photo and Vector; 12 Sergey Novikov; 13 Monkey Business Images; 13 George Rudy; 14 Svetography; 19 V9; 19 Sarawut panchawa; 19 Foamfoto; 19 Strelka; 19 Lisa S; 19 Fortovik; 20 Monticello; 21 Ritu Manoj Jethani; 22 Lapina; 24 Pavel Ilyukhin; 25 YanLev; 25 Doczky; 25 Goran Cakmazovic; 25 Lukasz Szwaj; 25 Timofeev Sergey; 25 Yuganov Konstantin; 25 Pavel L Photo and Video; 26 Nattika; 27 Natali Zakharova; 27 Mikhaylovskiy; 28 DayOwl; 29 Barbara Dudzinska; 29 Al1962; 32 Evgeny Bakharev; 33 Creativa Images; 33 Vira Mylyan-Monastyrska; 33 Johan Swanepoel; 33 Mylmages-Micha; 33 B Isnor; 33 Zossia; 34 Racheal Grazias; 35 Gloriole; 38 AnneMS; 39 Panu Ruangjan; 39 Jumnong; 39 Lightspring; 39 Johnnyraff; 39 Stefano Venturi; 39 Ondrej Prosicky; 40 Anna Hoychuk; 41 Leonardo Mercon; 41 Gaschwald; 41 Marktucan; 41 Sergey Moskvitin; 41 Aleksei Verhovski; 41 Jeep2499; 42 Katinka Bakos; 46 Valery Bareta; 47 2p2play; 48 Anneka; 49 Ociacia; 49 Vchal; 50 Nito; 50 Dymax; 50 Ekkapon; 50 Photo Melon; 50 Brian Kinney; 51 Iakov Filimonov; 52 EvgeniiAnd; 53 Gabriel12; 54 Pockethifi; 55 R.classen; 55 DenisNata; 56 Sergey Novikov; 60 Pete Saloutos; 61 Jiri Hera; 61 J. Helgason; 61 Neamov; 61 Drohn; 61 Nito; 61 Trekandshoot; 62 Mauricio Graiki; 63 Volodymyr Burdiak; 64 Volkovslava; 67 Christian Jung; 67 Mikkel Bigandt; 68 Jacek Chabraszewski; 69 Mario.lizaola; 69 Joannawnuk; 70 JaySi; 74 GRSI; 75 SpeedKingz; 75 Furtseff; 75 Lapandr; 75 Africa Studio; 75 Kozlik; 75 BortN66; 76 Koliadzynska Iryna; 77 Gillmar; 78 Sergey Nivens; 80 Romrodphoto; 81 Laptopnet; 81 PhotoJanski; 81 Dusan Milenkovic; 81 Vvita; 81 Poomooq; 81 SpongePo; 82 Travellight; 84 Dmytro Gilitukha; 84 Lapina; **Multiple pages (Ideas Focus)** Kaesler Media; **Multiple pages (Ideas Focus)** Kostudio; **Multiple pages (Review Pages)** Pikselstock; **Multiple pages (Review Pages)** Odua Images

Printed in the United Kingdom by Ashford Colour Press
Print Number: 11    Print Year: 2024

# Contents

## Reading

**A**   Read the *Exam Reminder*. What is the main topic of the texts in the *Exam Task*?

_____

**B**   Now complete the *Exam Task*.

Text 1

Exam Reminder

**Reading for main ideas**

- Read the heading to find out the main topic of the text. Then quickly read the text to find out more.
- Remember to read the text again and underline the main ideas.

Text 2

### My family and me!

I'm Anass and I'm 12 years old. I live in Morocco, in a place called El Khorbat in the mountains. It's very dry where I live. It doesn't rain very often, so we haven't got a lot of trees. It's usually hot, but in the winter it sometimes snows!

My family lives in a house in town. We have a garden with chickens and goats, and I give them food sometimes. I live with my mother and father, and I have two younger sisters. I don't have any brothers, but that's OK. I have lots of fun with my sisters!

My favourite activities are reading books and painting. My teacher at school gives us art assignments, and I like painting animals and my home and garden. My classmates and I put our paintings on the wall in class. Some paintings are very creative. I like going to school with my fellow students!

### My family life

I'm Gyrongav. I'm 12 years old and I live in Siberia, near the Arctic Ocean. My family and I are members of the Chukchi people of Eastern Russia. My name means 'spring' in the Chukchi language!

I live with my mother and father on a farm in a small village. I am an only child, but I want to have a baby sister one day. I have aunts, uncles and cousins, and my grandparents live near us, too.

My favourite activity is running races with my schoolmates! We run fast and try to be first to the finish line. I'm quite good, but I don't always win. I also like playing with my dolls and I love hearing my grandparents tell exciting stories about the past.

Read the two texts. Are sentences **1 – 8** 'Right' (**A**) or 'Wrong' (**B**)?

1  Anass and Gyrongav are almost teenagers. ☐
2  Anass and Gyrongav live in the same country. ☐
3  It is sometimes cold where Anass lives. ☐
4  Both Anass and Gyrongav have got sisters. ☐
5  Anass wants to have a brother. ☐
6  Anass and Gyrongav enjoy spending time with their classmates. ☐
7  A picture of Anass's house is in his classroom. ☐
8  Gyrongav likes having races with her family. ☐

# Vocabulary

**A**  Match these words to the photos.

> brother   dad   granddad   grandma   mum   sister

## My family tree

**Rose**

1 _____

**Jimmy**

2 _____

**Mary**

3 _____

**Alan**

4 _____

**Glen (Me!)**

**Jessica**

5 _____

**Stanley**

6 _____

**B**  Circle the correct words.

1  A watch / poster tells the time.
2  Jill's got lots of friends. She's very popular / married.
3  My mum's brother is my uncle / aunt.
4  This is Mr / Mrs Barnes. She's our maths teacher.
5  My aunt and uncle's kids are my cousins / sisters.
6  I have no brothers or sisters. I'm an alone / only child.

## C Complete the words for the photos.

**1** m _ _ _ _ _ _

**2** d _ _ _ _

**3** k _ _ _ _ _

**4** f _ _ _ _ _ _ _ b _ _ _ _

**5** n _ _ _ _ _ _ _

**6** f _ _ _ _ n _ _ _ _

## D Complete the text with these words.

> parents   photograph   poster   smartphone   surname   teenagers

Hi, I'm Yuri and I study English. I've got 17 classmates in my English class. We're **(1)** _____; my classmates and I are all 13 years old. Our teacher, Ms Alice, is 29 years old. Her **(2)** _____ is Holloway, but she likes Ms Alice better! ☺ I take English lessons because I like the language. Also, my **(3)** _____ want me to get a good job and English helps. I like our classroom; there's a large **(4)** _____ of Buckingham Palace on the wall. Can you believe the palace has 775 rooms? And 240 of them are bedrooms! That's big enough for everyone in my town to stay in it! Actually, my town is small – there are only 600 people. Our last class is next week and Ms Alice wants to take a **(5)** _____ of all of us. I'm going to take one using my **(6)** _____. I'm sad that the class is ending, but I'm excited about the summer. It's 90 days of no school or homework – or 2,160 hours of fun, if you want to look at it that way! ☺

## E Write the numbers in the text in D as words. Write them in the order they appear.

**1** _____     **5** _____

**2** _____     **6** _____

**3** _____     **7** _____

**4** _____     **8** _____

# Grammar

**Be; Have got; Questions with Be & Have got; This, That, These, Those; Possession**

**A** Complete the dialogue with the correct form of *be* or *have got*. Use contractions and negative forms where needed.

**Paula:** Hi, I (**1**) _____ Paula.

**Trevor:** Hi, Paula. Where (**2**) _____ you from?

**Paula:** Bogota, Colombia. My family (**3**) _____ Colombian. This (**4**) _____ my pet bird.

**Trevor:** (**5**) _____ your bird _____ a name?

**Paula:** Of course … Polly!

**Trevor:** I (**6**) _____ a pet, too – my dog, Franklin. He (**7**) _____ his own house in our back garden.

**Paula:** Nice! Polly (**8**) _____ my only family pet. We (**9**) _____ a turtle and a hamster as well.

**Trevor:** Wow, three pets! I (**10**) _____ three – only Franklin!

**B** Complete the questions for the responses with *be* or *have got*. Use a question word where needed.

**1 A:** _____?
**B:** My favourite colours are green, red and gold.

**2 A:** _____?
**B:** I'm from Malta.

**3 A:** _____?
**B:** I've got three aunts and three uncles.

**4 A:** _____ on his farm?
**B:** He's got two horses and three cows.

**5 A:** _____?
**B:** Their house has got ten rooms.

**6 A:** _____ new glasses?
**B:** Yes, I have.

**7 A:** _____?
**B:** Because a fish is a great pet!

**8 A:** _____ your best friends?
**B:** They are George and Marios.

**C** Complete the sentences with *this, that, these* or *those*.

**1** Do you like _____ shirt I'm wearing?

**2** _____ books next to me are mine. Your books are on the table.

**3** Do you hear _____ noise? I think it's outside.

**4** _____ here is a photograph of my trip to New York.

**5** _____ boots over there are quite nice.

**6** Can you bring me _____ board game, please?

**D** Choose the correct answers.

**1** Would you like to come to _____ birthday party?
  **a** your    **b** my

**2** Have the kids got _____ smartphones with them?
  **a** their    **b** its

**3** _____ and your brother are welcome here anytime.
  **a** Your    **b** You

**4** My _____ house in on the beach. I visit them every summer.
  **a** cousin's    **b** cousins'

**5** The _____ toilet is down the hall and to the left.
  **a** mens'    **b** men's

**6** My kitten's got _____ own little bed!
  **a** its    **b** it's

**7** This is a photograph of my uncle. You can see _____ farm behind him.
  **a** his    **b** her

**8** Do you like _____ new car? We really like driving it.
  **a** your    **b** our

**E** Complete the text with these words.

am   got   has   have   his   is   my   their   this   those

Hi, I **(1)** _____ Luke and **(2)** _____ photograph shows **(3)** _____ bedroom. I really like it and I spend a lot of time here. It's **(4)** _____ a nice view of the lake, and the room **(5)** _____ big and full of light. You can see that I **(6)** _____ got a skateboard and a football, and the football **(7)** _____ got cool red stars on it. I can see my friend Ron's house from the window. It's on the other side of the lake and **(8)** _____ house is very near the water. I've got some of his things in my room – **(9)** _____ books on the bookshelf are Ron's books. The alarm clock near my bed is a gift from my grandparents. **(10)** _____ gifts are always really useful!

# Listening

**Exam Reminder**

**A** Read the *Exam Reminder*. What words do speakers often use to correct information?

_____

**B** 1.1 ▶️ Listen and complete the *Exam Task*.

**Choosing the correct option**
- You will hear a long conversation and must match five pieces of information to seven choices in this task.
- The options are very similar, but only one is correct for each question.
- Words like *no*, *actually*, *but* and *in fact* tell you the speaker is going to correct information the other speaker gave. Listen for these words to help you choose the correct answers.

## Exam Task

Listen to a young girl talking about her family's favourite things. What item does each family member like the most? For questions **1 – 5**, write a letter **A – G** next to each item. You will hear the conversation twice.

| 1 | Thomas | ☐ | **A** clothes |
| 2 | Eric | ☐ | **B** video games |
| 3 | Anne | ☐ | **C** smartphone |
| 4 | Dad | ☐ | **D** necklace |
| 5 | Mum | ☐ | **E** camera |
| | | | **F** car |
| | | | **G** diary |

**C** 1.2 ▶️ Listen again and check your answers.

# Writing: a personal description

**A** **Some verbs in these sentences do not agree with the subject. Cross out the wrong verb and write the correct form.**

1 My family and I lives in Bern, Switzerland. _____
2 My sister has got a guitar and a violin. _____
3 My brother really love football and basketball. _____
4 I like the colour purple, but I don't like orange. _____
5 My cousin is 14 years old and I is, too! _____
6 My grandparents has got a house in Italy. _____

## Learning Reminder

**Writing about yourself**
- Make your descriptions more interesting by using different verbs.
- Check that the spelling of your verbs agrees with the subject of the sentence.
- Add information with the words *and*, *also* and *too*.
- Show contrast with the words *but* and *however*.

**B** **Replace the underlined words with these words or phrases.**

| but  however  listens to  live  love |

1 I <u>really like</u> skiing and snowboarding. _____
2 My aunt and uncle <u>are</u> in Berlin. _____
3 My best friend <u>has got</u> lots of different music. _____
4 I love the summer <u>and</u> I like the winter, too. _____
5 We live by a lake, <u>but</u> I don't swim in it. _____

**C** **Read the example email and tick (✓) the lines that you can use in a reply.**

*Remember to use 25–35 words in your reply.*

○○○        Email Message

From: Becky    To: Neil

Hi Neil,
I've got some news for you … I've got a new pet – a dog called Sammy! He's great fun. What are your favourite pets? What things can I do with Sammy? What things can't I do?
Write back soon!
Your friend,
Becky

*Underline the three questions.*

*Circle who you are writing to.*

1 Dear Neil, ☐
2 That's fantastic news! ☐
3 I don't like cats very much. ☐
4 You can take Sammy to the park. ☐
5 However, you can't leave him alone. ☐
6 Bye for now, ☐

**D** **Read and complete the *Exam Task*. Don't forget to use the *Useful Expressions* on page 15 of your Student's Book.**

## Exam Task

Read the email from your new teacher.

○○○        Email Message

From: Mr Larson
To: Year 7 Class

Dear students,

I'm Mr Larson, your new teacher, and I would like to learn about my students. Who's in your family? What do you do in your free time? What is your favourite thing? Bring a photo and your description to school and we'll put them on the class wall together.

Bye for now,

Mr Larson

Write an email to Mr Larson and answer the questions.

Write **25–35** words.

⟳ Writing Reference p. 170 in Student's Book

## Reading

**A** Read the *Exam Reminder*. What is the conversation in the *Exam Task* about?

_____

**B** Now complete the *Exam Task*.

### Exam Task

Complete the conversation. What does Marvin say to Scott? Choose the correct answer **A – G**. There are two letters you do not need to use.

**Scott:** What do you like doing online?

**Marvin:** (1) _____

**Scott:** Why do you watch skateboarding events?

**Marvin:** (2) _____

**Scott:** Do you go to these events, too?

**Marvin:** (3) _____

**Scott:** When's the next one?

**Marvin:** (4) _____

**Scott:** Do you go with anyone else?

**Marvin:** (5) _____

**A** I do skateboarding and go bike riding.

**B** I watch them because I think the sport is exciting.

**C** I think it's in a couple of weeks.

**D** I like playing games and watching skateboarding events.

**E** You can come with me sometime if you want.

**F** Yes, I do. I go twice a month.

**G** I do. My friend Oscar comes with me.

# Vocabulary

**A** Match these words to the photos.

boots   hoody   jeans   shorts   skirt   socks   trainers   trousers

1 _____

2 _____

3 _____

4 _____

5 _____

6 _____

7 _____

8 _____

**B** Complete the sentences with the correct form of *do*, *go* or *play*.

1 We can't _____ swimming today; it's raining.
2 Mike _____ judo at weekends with friends.
3 Can we _____ tennis at your local park?
4 Mum _____ running with a friend twice a week.
5 My whole family _____ basketball for a local team.
6 I don't like _____ chess.

**C** Circle the correct words.

1 Maria is sociable / patient; she talks to everyone.
2 Josh plays sport for two hours each day because he's quite creative / energetic.
3 My sister is patient / shy, so she doesn't meet a lot of people.
4 Lisa knows where all her stuff is because she's so organised / creative.
5 Beth has got on some sporty / energetic clothes; a colourful tracksuit and nice new trainers.
6 Michael and his best friend like painting a lot because they're shy / creative.

**D** Match the first parts of the sentences 1–6 to the second parts a–f.

1 We often have ☐
2 Leslie meets ☐
3 I want to go ☐
4 Michelle and Beth chat ☐
5 I don't get on ☐
6 We love to hang ☐

a up with her study group on Mondays.
b to each other online often.
c for lunch at the new burger place.
d with my classmates very well.
e out with our friends at the local café.
f fun with the neighbour's kids.

**E** Complete the text with these words. Use the *-ing* form where needed.

do   draw   go   listen   play   watch

My brother Bart and I like different things. He likes (**1**) _____ TV programmes, but I enjoy (**2**) _____ to music on my MP3 player. At the weekend, he often (**3**) _____ video games at his friend's house for hours. But me, I like (**4**) _____ out with my friends to a bookshop, the cinema or a park. I also love (**5**) _____ drama at school, but Bart thinks that's boring. The truth is Bart isn't a very creative person. However, sometimes he (**6**) _____ cartoon figures in his notebook. He's actually rather good at it!

# Grammar

## Present Simple for routines & habits; Negatives; *Yes / No* Questions & Short Answers; Question Words; Adverbs of Frequency; Time expressions

**A** Complete the sentences with the correct form of the verbs in brackets.

1 My class _____ (**start**) in about an hour.
2 My friends and I _____ (**play**) football on Wednesdays.
3 I _____ (**not do**) homework every day.
4 She _____ (**not chat**) online with her friends.
5 He _____ (**like**) both the cinema and the theatre.
6 Ms Jones _____ (**teach**) English to Polish students.
7 My parents _____ (**not go**) out very often.
8 Alex _____ (**see**) his grandparents once a month.

**B Complete the responses.**

1 A: Do you like going swimming?
B: Yes, _____.

2 A: Does your sister drive?
B: No, _____.

3 A: Do you and your friends play basketball?
B: Yes, _____.

4 A: Do your parents buy your clothes?
B: No, _____.

5 A: Do I look good in this T-shirt?
B: Yes, _____.

6 A: Does your class end this week?
B: No, _____.

**C Complete the questions. Use a question word, a subject and a verb.**

1 A: _____ at the weekend?
B: I hang out with friends or listen to music.

2 A: _____?
B: My best friend lives a few streets away from me.

3 A: _____ to online?
B: I chat to my friends and my cousins.

4 A: _____ tennis?
B: My sister and I play tennis on Wednesdays and Fridays.

5 A: _____ trainers all the time?
B: Because he likes the way they look.

6 A: _____ to your house?
B: Walk down Stanley Road as far as the bookshop and then turn right.

**D Write the words in the correct order to make sentences or questions.**

1 do / in / evenings / I / usually / the / homework / my
_____

2 go / with / We / sometimes / neighbours / out / our
_____

3 is / for / her / Janice / often / late / class
_____

4 Frank / never / socks / does / wear / Why / ?
_____

5 are / at / ever / They / home / hardly
_____

6 always / does / do / Henry / well / exams / in / How / ?
_____

**E Complete the text with these words. There are two words you do not need to use.**

| always | doesn't | don't | every | hardly | how | never | sometimes | twice | why |
|--------|---------|-------|-------|--------|-----|-------|-----------|-------|-----|

I love playing chess, but I (1) _____ play with my friends. They (2) _____ like playing it at all. They often ask me, '(3) _____ do you like playing chess?' I tell them that it's a clever game. It's not exciting like video games or basketball, but you really have to use your head. I usually play chess with my uncle, but I (4) _____ play with my granddad. I don't play chess (5) _____ day, of course. I usually play it once or (6) _____ a month. My uncle is quite good, but he (7) _____ always win! My granddad is very good and he (8) _____ ever loses.

# Listening

**A** Read the *Exam Reminder*. Who are the speakers in the *Exam Task* and what is the topic?

_____

**B** 2.1 ▷◁ **Listen and complete the *Exam Task*.**

## Exam Reminder

**Listening to instructions**

- The instructions identify the speaker and the topic, so listen carefully for these details.
- You will answer five questions and each question has three answer choices. Use the time at the beginning to read the questions quickly.

## Exam Task

You will listen to Aaron talking to his friend Monique about an after-school class.
For each question, choose the right answer (**a**, **b** or **c**). You will hear the conversation twice.

**1** Which class do Aaron and Monique choose?
  **a** yoga
  **b** photography
  **c** street dancing

**2** When will they go to the class?
  **a** Wednesday evenings
  **b** Friday evenings
  **c** Saturday afternoons

**3** What will Monique wear at the class?
  **a** trainers
  **b** her mum's shoes
  **c** sandals

**4** How much will they each pay?
  **a** £10
  **b** £18
  **c** £9

**5** What time will Aaron and Monique meet?
  **a** 6.00 p.m.
  **b** 5.30 p.m.
  **c** 7.00 p.m.

**C** 2.2 ▷◁ **Listen again and check your answers.**

# Writing: responding to an advert

**A** Match two questions to each advert.

## Learning Reminder

**Identifying who to write to for more information**

- Adverts give a few general details about products, events, classes or jobs.
- For specific information, we must contact the person or company or visit websites listed in the advert.

**1**

**Bookshelf for sale**
In good condition and a very good price. It would look great in a living room or bedroom. For more information, email me at dr123@fastmail.com.

**2**

**Cheap, fun holidays!**
**Three low-cost packages to central Europe – Czech Republic, Hungary and Austria. Have the time of your life at half the cost!**
**Visit our website at www.travelnow.com or email Ms Paula Stone at pstone@travelnow.com.**

**3**

**Homes for pets**
We're giving away some sweet, cute and very friendly kittens! Call 01 099284 for more information.

**4**

**Join a music club!**
We're a group of four musicians who love music and we're starting a new club. It's free to join – meet creative, sociable people and have fun! Email Josh at musicclub@onemail.com.

**a** How many days are they for?  _____
**b** What colour are they?  _____
**c** When does it start?  _____
**d** How big is it?  _____

**e** Where do you meet?  _____
**f** How much does it cost?  _____
**g** When do they begin?  _____
**h** How many are there?  _____

**B** Look at the adverts in A again and answer the questions.

1 Which advert tells you to contact someone by phone? _____
2 For which advert are there two ways to find out more information? _____
3 For which advert do you begin an email with 'Dear Sir or Madam'? _____
4 For which adverts do you know the costs? _____
5 In which advert does the contact have a title (e.g. *Mr*) before their name? _____
6 Which advert gives you a website to go to for more information? _____

**C** Complete the email in response to this advert with these words and phrases. There are some words or phrases you do not need to use.

beginners   best wishes   bye for now   cost   Greg   information   last   Mr Osmond   Sir   website design

Begin formal emails with **Dear Sir** or **Dear Madam**, and end with **Yours faithfully**.

### Website design class

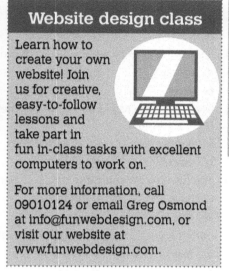

Learn how to create your own website! Join us for creative, easy-to-follow lessons and take part in fun in-class tasks with excellent computers to work on.

For more information, call 09010124 or email Greg Osmond at info@funwebdesign.com, or visit our website at www.funwebdesign.com.

If you know the name and surname, begin with **Dear Mr/Mrs Osmond**. If you don't know if a woman is married, use **Ms**.

● ○ ○            Email Message

Dear (1) _____,
I would like more
(2) _____ about
the website design class. How much does the class
(3) _____?
Do you have lessons for
(4) _____?
How long does each lesson
(5) _____?
(6) _____,
Lily Reinhart

**D** Read and complete the *Exam Task*. Don't forget to use the *Useful Expressions* on page 27 of your Student's Book.

## Exam Task

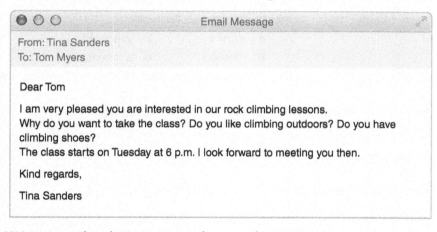

Read the email from the instructor of a climbing class.

● ○ ○            Email Message

From: Tina Sanders
To: Tom Myers

Dear Tom

I am very pleased you are interested in our rock climbing lessons.
Why do you want to take the class? Do you like climbing outdoors? Do you have climbing shoes?
The class starts on Tuesday at 6 p.m. I look forward to meeting you then.

Kind regards,

Tina Sanders

Write an email to the instructor and answer the questions.
Write **25–35** words.

↻ Writing Reference p. 171 in Student's Book

# Vocabulary

**A** Choose the correct answers.

1 I'm 11 and my _____ Tom is nine.
   **a** uncle    **c** granddad
   **b** father    **d** brother

2 My sister and I _____ a coffee sometimes.
   **a** go out    **c** hang out
   **b** have fun    **d** go for

3 My _____ Helena is my dad's sister.
   **a** sister    **c** aunt
   **b** mother    **d** grandma

4 My address is 47 Homer St. We write the number as _____.
   **a** forty-seven    **c** four-seven
   **b** four-seventy    **d** fourteen-seven

5 Her first name is Kylie, but I don't know her _____.
   **a** name    **c** surname
   **b** first    **d** names

6 I've got a _____ of Daniel Radcliffe on my wall.
   **a** shirt    **c** poster
   **b** diary    **d** watch

7 I'm very _____. Can I have another sandwich?
   **a** patient    **c** hungry
   **b** energetic    **d** sporty

8 Your _____ looks very warm!
   **a** sweatshirt    **c** watch
   **b** necklace    **d** poster

9 Mark is _____, so he hasn't got many friends.
   **a** patient    **c** organised
   **b** shy    **d** sociable

10 Do you know how to play a(n) _____?
   **a** dance    **c** chess
   **b** drama    **d** instrument

11 I often take pictures with my _____.
   **a** smartphone    **c** watch
   **b** tennis    **d** photograph

12 Paul doesn't like art. He's not very _____.
   **a** creative    **c** energetic
   **b** sporty    **d** organised

13 It's a good idea to wear _____ for running.
   **a** trainers    **c** boots
   **b** jeans    **d** watches

14 My _____ are Maria and George. They are my mum's parents.
   **a** aunts    **c** grandparents
   **b** cousins    **d** children

15 You have to be energetic to _____ street dance.
   **a** have    **c** play
   **b** go    **d** do

16 Jonathan _____ swimming at his local pool.
   **a** plays    **c** does
   **b** goes    **d** wears

17 I like being _____, so my desk is very clean.
   **a** sporty    **c** patient
   **b** sociable    **d** organised

18 Do you get _____ your brothers and sisters?
   **a** to    **c** on with
   **b** up    **d** with

19 I'm 13 now, so I'm finally _____!
   **a** a child    **c** years old
   **b** married    **d** a teenager

20 I often _____ up with my friends at my local park.
   **a** go    **c** hang
   **b** get    **d** meet

# Grammar

**B  Choose the correct answers.**

**1** My best friends _____ Jim and Stuart.

  **a** is          **c** are

  **b** has        **d** am

**2** '_____ any aunts or uncles?'
'Yes, I've got two of each.'

  **a** Have you        **c** You've got

  **b** You have        **d** Have you got

**3** I'm Henry and this is _____ brother, James.

  **a** me           **c** his

  **b** my          **d** its

**4** The _____ toys are all over the floor.

  **a** child's       **c** children's

  **b** children     **d** child

**5** 'Can I help you, miss?'
'Yes, I want to look at _____ boots over there.'

  **a** that         **c** these

  **b** those       **d** this

**6** _____ rooms has your house got?

  **a** How many    **c** When

  **b** How          **d** Where

**7** My sister and I _____ at our school.

  **a** sport play    **c** play sport

  **b** plays sport   **d** sport plays

**8** '_____ do you watch TV?'
'I watch it in the evenings, after studying.'

  **a** What        **c** When

  **b** Why         **d** Where

**9** 'Do you ride a bicycle often?'
'_____.'

  **a** Yes, I have    **c** Yes, I ride

  **b** Yes, I do      **d** Yes, I am

**10** 'Is _____ chair here new?'
'No, it just looks like it.'

  **a** this          **c** that

  **b** these       **d** those

**11** Mary _____ with her friend Sue online in the evening.

  **a** chat usually     **c** usually chats

  **b** usually chat     **d** chats usually

**12** 'How often do you listen to music?'
'I listen to music _____ day.'

  **a** at the        **c** every

  **b** in the        **d** once

**13** I _____ late for class.

  **a** am not often    **c** not am often

  **b** often am not    **d** not often am

**14** Julie _____ her sister's pet.

  **a** don't like      **c** not like

  **b** doesn't like    **d** does not

**15** 'Where do your new neighbours live?'
'_____ house is the red one with the white door.'

  **a** Their        **c** They're

  **b** They        **d** There

**16** The _____ desks are clean and ready for them.

  **a** students     **c** students'

  **b** student      **d** student's

**17** I _____ go to the theatre – only twice a year.

  **a** often        **c** always

  **b** hardly ever   **d** usually

**18** 'Are you from Colombia?'
'Yes, _____.'

  **a** I do         **c** I am

  **b** I'm          **d** I have

**19** 'What _____ name?'
'I call him Sam.'

  **a** is your pet's    **c** your pet's is

  **b** your is       **d** is your

**20** 'Does Lisa enjoy her new job?'
'No, she _____.'

  **a** isn't         **c** don't

  **b** hasn't       **d** doesn't

# Reading

**A** Read the *Exam Reminder*. Can you find words in the *Exam Task* sentences that are similar or connected to words in the notices?

_____

**B** Now complete the *Exam Task*.

## Exam Reminder

**Using words you know to understand signs**

- This part of the exam has sentences that you match to signs. There are five sentences and seven signs.
- Look for words in the signs or notices that you know. It's OK if you don't know all the words.
- Before you write your answer, compare each sentence to each sign.

## Exam Task

Which notice (**A – G**) says this (**1 – 5**)? There are two signs you don't need.

1 You cannot make calls here. ☐
2 You go in here to watch a sports match. ☐
3 You can do something with a present here. ☐
4 You cannot talk to people here. ☐
5 You can get two of something for the price of one here. ☐

A NO PARKING HERE

B USE PHONE IN CASE OF EMERGENCY

C QUIET PLEASE

D PLEASE TURN OFF MOBILE PHONES

E Gift-wrapping available here

F BUY 1 GET 1 FREE!

G STADIUM ENTRANCE

# Vocabulary

**A** Complete the words for the places.

1 s _____

2 h _____

3 r _____

4 t _____

5 s _____

6 l _____

**B** Match these words to make collocations. Then complete the sentences.

| fire (x2)  football  police (x2)  shop | assistant  fighter  match  officer  station (x2) |

1 You tell a _____ when you see a crime.
2 Fire engines leave a _____ when there is a fire.
3 You watch a _____ in a stadium.
4 A _____ helps to stop a fire.
5 When you buy clothes, a _____ helps you find things.
6 If you do something bad, you may have to go to a _____.

**C** Unjumble the words and complete the sentences.

acercrseou  ernsu  etwari  lagivel  octar  riblinara  tpecorsats  ycit

1 The _____ will bring your medicine in a minute.
2 Where is the _____? I want another fizzy drink.
3 There are thousands of _____ in the stadium right now.
4 My uncle lives in a small _____ about an hour from my house.
5 You can ask the _____ to help you find books.
6 My father goes to the _____ every month, but his horse never wins.
7 I know that _____ – he's in a very popular play.
8 London is a big _____ and it's easy to get lost.

**D** Circle the correct words.

1 This is our stop, so let's get on / get off the bus.
2 My mum takes / drives a train to get to her office in the city.
3 Let's ride / drive our bikes to school today. It's a nice day.
4 Dad leaves work at five and arrives / arrives at home 30 minutes later.
5 Lisa, get in / get on the car now – we need to go!
6 Don't miss / catch the bus or you'll be late.

## Exam Reminder

**E** Read the *Exam Reminder*.
Then complete the *Exam Task*.

**Reviewing vocabulary**
- For this task, you will read definitions for five words. The words belong to the same topic. You will see the first letter of the word and the gaps for the rest of the letters in the word.
- Look back at the vocabulary for each unit and make word maps for each topic. Test yourself or a classmate on spelling.

## Exam Task

Read the descriptions of things that you can buy. What is the word for each one? The first letter is already there. There is **one** space for **each letter** in the word.

1 This is something that swims in the sea.     f _ _ _
2 These are things you read.                    b _ _ _ _ _
3 You buy this at a butcher's shop.             m _ _ _
4 These are plants and you eat them.            v _ _ _ _ _ _ _ _ _
5 This helps you feel better when you're sick.  m _ _ _ _ _ _ _

# Grammar

## *There is / There are; Prepositions; Present Continuous*

**A** Complete the sentences with *there is/isn't, there are/aren't* or *Is/Are there*.

1 _____ three chemist's shops in my neighbourhood.
2 _____ a good restaurant near your house?
3 _____ a library here, so we have to go to the city centre.
4 _____ any good films showing at the cinema tonight?
5 If you want a good bakery, _____ one on Candlestick Road.
6 _____ six eggs in the box. We only have five.

**B Circle the correct words.**

1 Don't step back … there's someone in front of / behind you.
2 There's a bank under / opposite the police station. You have to cross the street.
3 Do you know who's sitting next to / on our teacher?
4 Can you see where I am? I'm standing under / in front of the fire station.
5 It's really warm today. Let's eat in / on the garden.
6 I've got an idea where your cat is. He's hiding on / under my bed.

**C Complete the sentences with the correct Present Continuous form of these verbs.**

1 I _____ (put) my new clothes in my wardrobe.
2 We _____ (leave) the library to go home right now.
3 He _____ (make) lunch for his family at the moment.
4 _____ (you / do) your homework now or after dinner?
5 They _____ (not talk) to each other these days.
6 Why _____ (rain) so much today? I want the sun!

**D Choose the correct answer.**

1 I can't talk. We _____ an exam at the moment.
   a 're not having    b 're having
2 Lisa _____ for work at 7 a.m. tomorrow morning.
   a 're leaving    b 's leaving
3 They _____ a programme on TV right now.
   a 's watching    b 're watching
4 I'm telling you the story, but you _____!
   a 're not listening    b 're listening
5 _____ in the evenings these days?
   a You are studying    b Are you studying
6 _____ fun at the party?
   a Are they having    b They aren't having

**E Read the *Exam Reminder* and complete the *Exam Task*.**

Exam Task

Read a student's description of a photograph. Choose the best word (**a**, **b** or **c**) for each space.

**My favourite photo**

This is a photograph of the Brooklyn public library. It is (**1**) _____ my aunt and uncle's house, so it's very easy to walk there. It is similar (**2**) _____ some buildings in my home town of Athens and that's why I like it. (**3**) _____ is a lot of space inside the building for reading books in peace and quiet. I often visit this library (**4**) _____ the summer because this is when I stay (**5**) _____ my aunt and uncle. Also, I really enjoy spending my free time reading books. There (**6**) _____ many books on American history on the shelves, which I enjoy reading the most. At the moment, I (**7**) _____ about the 1800s in the US. It's an interesting time although many things today are different (**8**) _____ that time in history. I think I prefer today, but it's still great to read about the past!

| | | | | | |
|---|---|---|---|---|---|
| 1 | a | next | b | near | c | front |
| 2 | a | to | b | from | c | with |
| 3 | a | That | b | It | c | There |
| 4 | a | on | b | in | c | at |
| 5 | a | with | b | around | c | to |
| 6 | a | am | b | is | c | are |
| 7 | a | read | b | am reading | c | reads |
| 8 | a | in | b | with | c | from |

Exam Reminder

**Using prepositions**
- This part of the exam contains a short text with eight gaps. Each gap has three options.
- The gaps sometimes need prepositions.
- After you choose your answer, read the sentence with the other two options to check that they are wrong.

BROOKLYN PUBLIC LIBRARY

# Listening

**A** Read the *Exam Reminder*. Who is speaking in the *Exam Task* and what are they speaking about?

_____

**B** 🔊 3.1 Listen and complete the *Exam Task*.

## Exam Reminder

**Reading & listening to instructions**
- For this part of the exam, you will listen to two people having a conversation.
- Before beginning the task, listen to the instructions carefully to find out who is speaking and what they're going to speak about.
- Then look at the gaps in the text to find out what information you need to listen for.

## Exam Task

You will hear a man asking a female waiter about a restaurant. Listen and complete each question. You will hear the conversation twice.

**Birthday party at restaurant**

Location:
47 Danford Rd, near the (1) _____

Open from:
11 a.m. to (2) _____ p.m.,
Tuesday – Sunday

Closed on:
(3) _____

Number in group:
(4) _____ people coming

Name of group:
(5) _____

**C** 🔊 3.2 Listen again and check your answers.

# writing: an email

**A** Write sentences and questions with the correct form of these words and any other words you need.

1 I / want / visit / a castle / tomorrow

_____

2 we / can / meet / opposite / train station

_____

3 you / need / bring / money / ticket

_____

4 you / want / see / play / theatre / ?

_____

5 we / need / arrive / early / ?

_____

6 you / can / buy / tickets / stadium / ?

_____

## Learning Reminder

**Recognising verb patterns**
- When learning new verbs, try to learn the form of any verbs that follow it.
- These are some common verb forms:
  **need** + **to** + verb: *I need to finish my studies.*
  **can** + verb: *You can learn more about it online.*
  **want** + **to** + verb: *We want to go sightseeing.*

**B** Match the information to the sentences.

1 Let's see the afternoon show. ☐
2 I've got the £10 for the ticket. ☐
3 We can meet half an hour early … at 1.30 p.m. ☐
4 You can get it on offer this weekend. ☐
5 I want to leave in the morning. ☐
6 The bus gets us to Lisa's house by 8 p.m. ☐

a Flights to Paris: 8 a.m. –11 a.m. – 5.30 p.m.
b Walton Books – half price on many titles, this Saturday and Sunday only.
c *Inception*, 1 p.m. – 4.30 p.m. – 8 p.m.
d City tours, £8 (£6 for students & seniors). Bus leaves at 2 p.m.
e Travel to Brighton: train arrives 5.30 p.m., bus 7.45 p.m.
f Man United vs Chelsea, starts 7 p.m., £12 (£2 off for students)

**C** Read the two texts and answer the questions.

Look at both texts to complete gaps in the third text.

**Day trips for 4th July:**

– Lipton Falls: 5 hours 30 mins. Bus leaves at 2 p.m., returns at 7.30 p.m. Price: £18.50
– Resling National Park: 3 hrs 20 mins. Bus leaves at 11.30 a.m., returns at 2.50 p.m. Price: £15.50
– Mt Shasta: 9 hours. Bus leaves at 7 a.m., returns 4 p.m. Price: £21

*Ticket prices include meals. £2 off for students, £4 off for seniors (aged 55 and up).

Hi Fran. I want to do Mt Shasta. It's a big trip, I know, but it will be fun. I'm glad they've got student prices for us. My gran will come with us, too. She's great fun! Let's meet at the travel office at 6.30 a.m. Don't be late!

Symbols such as €, $ and £ tell you about prices.

Check for a.m. and p.m. to locate times and st, nd, rd and th for dates.

1 Which trip are they taking? _____
2 How long does that trip last? _____
3 Where are they going to meet? _____
4 When are they going to meet? _____
5 How much does Fran's ticket cost? _____
6 How much does her gran's ticket cost? _____

**D** Read and complete the *Exam Task*. Don't forget to use the *Useful Expressions* on page 41 of your Student's Book.

## Exam Task

Read the email and the bookshop poster. Donald and Thomas are school friends. Fill in the information in Donald's email to Thomas.

○○○       Email Message

Hi Donald,
Thanks for coming with me to the book signing. You're going to enjoy it, I promise! Let's meet at the bus stop near my house at 1.30 p.m. and we can go from there. The book *Up, Up and Away* is his best work. That's the one you want. You buy the book and he signs it, which I'm sure you know!
Talk to you soon,
Thomas

○○○       Email Message

Hey Thomas,
The event at (1) _____ Books for the book signing with (2) _____ is tomorrow. Are we still meeting at the (3) _____ like you say, at (4) _____ p.m.? I'm bringing (5) £ _____ for the book. I'm looking forward to the event!
Bye for now,
Donald

**Meet the Author!**

Flashlight Books presents a book signing with author Marty Glee. Mr Glee is signing his new book, *Space Race* (normally £25, special price of £18 during signing). We are proud to offer Mr Glee's other books, *Countdown to Mars* and *Up, Up and Away*, for the special price of £15 and £12.50.

Saturday, 23rd July, 2 p.m. – 4 p.m.
Flashlight Books
23 Hamilton St

⟳ Writing Reference p. 172 in Student's Book ▶

## Reading

**A** Read the *Exam Reminder*. What words should you underline in each sentence of the *Exam Task*?

_____

**B** Now complete the *Exam Task*.

# Carnival in Brazil!

In February in my home country of Brazil, we celebrate Carnival! During Carnival, many Brazilians go into the streets in fancy dress and they dance. We also play music and have a great time. Carnival doesn't only happen in Brazil. Many countries around the world have a carnival. But our carnival is the largest one. Almost five million people come out to celebrate in my home town of Rio de Janeiro! There is a lot of dancing during Carnival because the samba schools take part in parades. A samba school is a school where you learn how to dance the samba. The samba is a type of Brazilian dance. It's very popular in Brazil, but it's actually from Africa. During Carnival, the dancers wear amazing costumes and dance the samba through the streets. There are different schools, and the best costumes and dancers win prizes. My sister does the samba during Carnival, but I just go in fancy dress. This year I'm going as a boxer. I've got a cool pair of red gloves and some boxing shorts ready. It's going to be great fun!

## Exam Task

Read the text about a boy, Pedro, and a celebration in Brazil. Choose the best answer (**a**, **b** or **c**) for each question.

**1** The celebration happens in March.
  **a** Right  **b** Wrong  **c** Doesn't say

**2** Brazil and other countries put on a carnival.
  **a** Right  **b** Wrong  **c** Doesn't say

**3** The carnival in Pedro's home town is very big.
  **a** Right  **b** Wrong  **c** Doesn't say

**4** Pedro goes to a samba school.
  **a** Right  **b** Wrong  **c** Doesn't say

**5** The samba dance is not from Brazil.
  **a** Right  **b** Wrong  **c** Doesn't say

**6** Pedro's sister is a dancer in Carnival.
  **a** Right  **b** Wrong  **c** Doesn't say

**7** Pedro wants to be a real boxer.
  **a** Right  **b** Wrong  **c** Doesn't say

# Vocabulary

**A** Complete the invitation with *at* or *in*.

## HALLOWEEN PARTY! 🎃

What's the best celebration **(1)** _____ autumn? It's Halloween, of course!
So I'm having a party and you're invited! It starts **(2)** _____ seven
**(3)** _____ the evening and we will leave the house **(4)** _____
half past nine to go trick or treating. Then, **(5)** _____ midnight, we will
watch a scary movie. Since the party's **(6)** _____ the weekend, we don't
have school the next day and we can stay up late. You can sleep at my house.
My mum can take you home **(7)** _____ the morning. Hope to see you
**(8)** _____ the party!

**B** Complete the words for the photos.

1 w _____ c _____

2 c _____

3 b _____

4 b _____

5 f _____

6 f _____ d _____

**C** Complete the sentences with these words.

| barbecue | birthday card | Christmas tree | decorations | traditional clothes | wedding dress |

1 Oh, no! My _____ is dirty. I can't get married in this!
2 Let's put up lots of colourful _____ for the party.
3 People in the village wear _____ for some celebrations.
4 Put your name on the _____ so Sarah knows who it's from.
5 We put lights on our _____ and it looks very pretty at night.
6 The food on the _____ isn't ready yet, but the kids are really hungry!

**D** Put the words in brackets in the correct gaps. There is one word you do not need to use.

1 Let's _____ a barbecue this weekend. I'll also _____ some food in the kitchen.
(**make; have; get**)

2 I usually _____ a present from everyone I _____ an invitation to.
(**have; get; give**)

3 Can I _____ some cake? I can _____ a piece myself. (**have; make; get**)

4 For this special day, we all _____ traditional clothes and _____ traditional songs.
(**sing; make; wear**)

5 We can _____ lunch at a café if you like, or I can _____ dinner for you at home.
(**have; give; make**)

6 You can _____ a card for your gran, or you can just _____ her some flowers.
(**give; have; get**)

**E** Match the words to the definitions.

1 This is a funny-looking fruit that is yellow inside. ☐
2 This is a big orange fruit that's popular at Halloween. ☐
3 This is a small, scary animal with eight legs. ☐
4 It can be quite warm during this time of year. ☐
5 This fruit is very hard on the outside and white on the inside. ☐
6 This is a line of people dancing or walking. ☐
7 This vegetable is brown and white, and it grows in the ground. ☐
8 This is a light in a container. ☐
9 It can snow during this time of year. ☐
10 This is something that comes from a fruit or vegetable and you drink it. ☐

a coconut
b spider
c lantern
d pineapple
e pumpkin
f juice
g winter
h potato
i summer
j procession

# Grammar

## Present Simple & Present Continuous; Countable & Uncountable Nouns; Quantifiers

**A** Circle the correct words.

1 We are often wearing / often wear colourful dresses for this celebration.
2 Are we lighting / Do we light the fireworks now?
3 Dad is cooking / cooks meat on the barbecue at the moment.
4 Mum can't come to the phone because she makes / is making a cake.
5 Where are Shane and Helen? Are they riding / Do they ride the Ferris wheel?
6 He usually invites / is usually inviting a lot of people to his birthday parties.
7 I can't come over tonight; I am studying / study for a history exam.
8 Is she eating / Does she eat a sandwich or a hamburger? I can't see.

**B** Choose the correct answers.

1  I would like _____ bread with my meal, please.
   **a** any      **b** a      **c** some

2  Is there _____ ketchup in the fridge?
   **a** any      **b** some      **c** a

3  Would you like _____ orange as well as a sandwich?
   **a** an      **b** a      **c** any

4  Let's listen to _____ music, shall we?
   **a** any      **b** some      **c** a

5  Are there _____ eggs in the kitchen?
   **a** some      **b** an      **c** any

6  There is _____ university in my home town.
   **a** a      **b** an      **c** some

7  I've got _____ decorations to put up in the room.
   **a** some      **b** a      **c** any

8  Do you know _____ man called Mr Bean?
   **a** some      **b** any      **c** a

**C** Complete the sentences with *many, much, lot* or *lots*.

1  Do you see a _____ of tourists in your area?

2  There isn't _____ information about this festival.

3  How _____ invitations have you got for the wedding?

4  Frank has got _____ cousins – 13 in all!

5  There are _____ of activities to do around town, so have fun!

6  How _____ time do we have before the party starts?

7  I haven't got a _____ of money with me; let's go to the cash machine.

8  We've got _____ of confetti to throw when the birthday boy arrives.

**D** Complete the table with these words.

apple   child   coffee   confetti   cookie   festival   food   meat   money   plate   song   time
traffic   weather   woman

| Countable | Uncountable |
|---|---|
|  |  |

**E** Circle the correct words to complete the phone conversation.

**Jill:** Hi Beth. How are you?

**Beth:** I'm fine, thanks. I (**1**) 'm making / make sandwiches for tomorrow's party.

**Jill:** Oh, do you need (**2**) a / some help? I can come over.

**Beth:** Well, yes, if it isn't any trouble. I haven't got (**3**) some / any meat, actually. Can you bring some?

**Jill:** Sure. We've got (**4**) lots / lot of things in our fridge, such as meat, cheese and mustard. We haven't got (**5**) much / any bread, though. Only a few slices.

**Beth:** The meat is fine, thanks.

**Jill:** How (**6**) many / much people are coming to the party?

**Beth:** I think there will be around 20 guests, mostly family. It's my mum's birthday. We (**7**) 're having / have a big party every year. It's great fun. Why don't you come? It's tomorrow at 3 p.m.

**Jill:** That sounds great. I'd love to. So, I (**8**) bring / 'm bringing the meat to you now. Let's talk more when I'm there. I want to get your mum a present. What's (**9**) a / an exciting gift I can get her?

**Beth:** You can just get her (**10**) some / many nice flowers if you want. But you don't have to get her anything!

**Jill:** It's fine – I want to! So, see you in a minute.

**Beth:** OK, bye now!

# Listening

**A** Read the *Exam Reminder*. What types of numbers do the gaps in the *Exam Task* need?

_____

**B** ◖4.1▷◗ Listen and complete the *Exam Task*.

### Exam Reminder

**Listening for specific & detailed information**

- Before you begin, look at the gaps and decide what type of information you need to complete. There are often times, dates, days and numbers.
- Write answers while you listen the first time.
- Then check your answers while you listen the second time and correct any errors.

## Exam Task

You will hear a man on the radio talking about a town fair. Listen and complete each question.
You will hear the conversation twice.

**Kipling Town Fair**

Dates:
the 28th to the (1) _____ of April

Kids' activities:
a (2) _____ party, games and rides

Food:
traditional food, sweets and a (3) _____

Special Saturday event:
a display of (4) _____

For more information:
call (5) _____

**C** ◖4.2▷◗ Listen again and check your answers.

# Writing: a recipe

**A** Complete the recipe with these sequencers. Sometimes there is more than one answer.

After that   Finally   First   Next   Then

### Learning Reminder

**Using sequencers**

- Words like *First*, *Then*, *Next*, *After that* and *Finally* help your reader to know the order of the actions.
- You can use the imperative when you write a recipe, as well as when you write instructions or directions, e.g. **boil** the eggs.

Recipe for garlic bread:

Ingredients: garlic, butter, slices of bread

- (1) _____, put butter and garlic in a pan on the cooker.
- (2) _____, cook the butter and garlic for a few minutes.
- (3) _____, place one side of a slice of bread in the butter.
- (4) _____, put that slice on a baking sheet, butter side up.
- (5) _____, repeat with the other slices of bread until the baking sheet is full.
- (6) _____, bake the bread for 5–10 minutes until it's golden brown. Enjoy!

**B** Put the steps to these recipes in the correct order. After you finish, read the whole recipe to check that it makes sense.

*Recipe for green salad:*

*Ingredients: lettuce, tomatoes, onions, dressing*

*a   Finally, mix really well and serve!* ☐

*b   First, wash the lettuce very well.* ☐

*c   Next, chop the lettuce and put it in a bowl.* ☐

*d   After that, wash and chop the tomatoes and onions.* ☐

*e   Then, dry the lettuce to get rid of the water.* ☐

*f   Add the tomatoes, onions and dressing to the lettuce.* ☐

**Recipe for easy spaghetti:**

Ingredients: packet of spaghetti, tomato sauce, cheese

**a**   Stir the spaghetti and the sauce very well. ☐

**b**   Then, put the tomato sauce in another pan and cook it while the spaghetti cooks. ☐

**c**   After ten minutes of boiling, put the spaghetti in a strainer. ☐

**d**   Finally, serve the spaghetti on a plate and add cheese. Enjoy! ☐

**e**   First, put the spaghetti in boiling water. ☐

**f**   Next, put the spaghetti in a big bowl and pour the sauce over it. ☐

**C** Read the email and decide if the sentences are true (T) or false (F).

*There is often more than one time, number or date, so read carefully to choose the correct one.*

Email Message

Hi Roger,
How are you? I'm writing a to-do list for the party. It starts at 3 p.m. and Sarah is coming an hour early to help set things up. I'm making lasagne, which takes a couple of hours to make. I'm making that early so it will be hot and ready when the party starts. Can you bring some chairs for outside? I've only got six and we need chairs for eight people.
Thanks,
Beth

*Think about phrases such as an hour early to help you write correct times in your answers.*

*Abbreviations such as a.m. and p.m. tell you if it's morning or afternoon/evening.*

1   Roger is writing a to-do list. ☐
2   The party begins in the afternoon. ☐
3   Sarah is arriving at 2 p.m. ☐
4   Sarah is going to do some cooking. ☐
5   Beth will start making the lasagne at 2 p.m. ☐
6   Beth asks Roger to bring eight chairs. ☐

**D** Read and complete the *Exam Task*. Don't forget to use the *Useful Expressions* on page 53 of your Student's Book.

## Exam Task

Read Donna's email to Connie and the to-do list. Fill in the information on Connie's text message to her friend.

Email Message

Hi Connie,
I'm looking forward to our picnic! The weather's going to be 20 degrees and sunny – very nice! Listen, I can't bring sandwiches, but I can get drinks and a cake. I'm going to be a bit late, probably about 30 minutes late. Georgina says that she's going to bring crisps.
Bye for now,
Donna

**To-do list – picnic at Central Park**

– Make sandwiches and a salad.     – Get some crisps. ✓ (Georgina)

– Bring drinks. ✓ (Connie)          – Tell Georgina to bring her music player.

Hi Georgina. About the picnic at (1) _____ – we're still meeting at 1 p.m., but Donna won't get there until (2) _____. She's bringing drinks and a (3) _____ and she says you're bringing crisps. I'm making sandwiches and a (4) _____. Can you bring your (5) _____? See you there!

⟳ Writing Reference p. 173 in Student's Book

# Vocabulary

**A Choose the correct answers.**

1 You can buy this medicine at the _____.
   a butcher's        c greengrocer's
   b chemist's        d bookshop

2 The bus is coming … don't _____ it!
   a miss        c ride
   b catch        d get

3 A(n) _____ takes you to hospital.
   a waiter        c ambulance
   b fire fighter        d shop assistant

4 We like to watch scary films _____ night.
   a by        c for
   b at        d in

5 Let's put some colourful _____ on the wall.
   a pumpkins        c decorations
   b spiders        d flowers

6 In this part of the celebration, everybody _____ hands.
   a holds        c watches
   b has        d wears

7 Let's _____ a nice bonfire this evening.
   a visit        c have
   b get        d give

8 The leaves turn to red, yellow and brown in _____.
   a autumn        c summer
   b winter        d spring

9 The kids want a large birthday _____ for the party.
   a juice        c meat
   b cake        d sweets

10 We're having _____ in our garden at the weekend.
   a a fair        c lights
   b presents        d a barbecue

11 Let's throw _____ at the wedding party!
   a fireworks        c cards
   b decorations        d confetti

12 The _____ is coming to see you about your illness.
   a officer        c nurse
   b actor        d spectator

13 Tina goes to the _____ every day to read books.
   a stadium        c library
   b theatre        d hospital

14 We're getting something to eat from the _____.
   a police station        c fishmonger's
   b fire station        d chemist's

15 You have to tell a _____ about the crime!
   a police officer        c fire fighter
   b spectator        d nurse

16 This is my bus stop. I _____ here and ride the bus to school.
   a drive        c get off
   b arrive at        d get on

17 Do you live in a big _____ like London?
   a town        c house
   b village        d city

18 We go swimming in the _____ when it's very hot.
   a winter        c autumn
   b spring        d summer

19 I have to wake up so early _____ the morning.
   a on        c at
   b by        d in

20 I hope we see lots of _____ in the sky for the celebration this year.
   a cakes        c presents
   b fireworks        d tricks

# Grammar

**B** Choose the correct answers.

1 _____ some pencils on the teacher's desk.
   **a** Is there    **c** There are
   **b** Are there    **d** There is

2 'Where can I find a room for the night near here?'
   '_____ a hotel in the square.'
   **a** It's    **c** It
   **b** There    **d** There's

3 'What are you wearing to the dance?'
   'I _____ a black and yellow dress.'
   **a** wear    **c** wearing
   **b** wears    **d** 'm wearing

4 'When do you celebrate Carnival?'
   'We _____ it in February.'
   **a** are celebrating    **c** is celebrating
   **b** celebrate    **d** celebrates

5 Have you got _____ milk in your fridge?
   **a** an    **c** lots
   **b** a    **d** any

6 There _____ juice on the kitchen table.
   **a** is any    **c** are some
   **b** are any    **d** is some

7 This restaurant has got _____ healthy food
   on the menu.
   **a** lot    **c** lot of
   **b** a lot    **d** lots of

8 'It's time to eat. I'm very hungry!'
   'OK. How _____ slices of pizza do you want?'
   **a** many    **c** much
   **b** any    **d** some

9 I'm afraid there isn't _____ food to eat.
   **a** some    **c** much
   **b** many    **d** lots

10 'Are there any balloons outside?'
   'Yes, there _____ around the table.'
   **a** are any    **c** is some
   **b** is any    **d** are some

11 Today our neighbour _____ a big party.
   **a** is having    **c** has
   **b** are having    **d** have

12 'What's your dad doing right now?'
   'He _____ the car in the car park.'
   **a** parking    **c** parks
   **b** is parking    **d** park

13 'We're at the party now.'
   '_____ people there?'
   **a** There are many    **c** Is there much
   **b** There is much    **d** Are there many

14 '_____ you to the concert?'
   'No, he isn't.'
   **a** Does Dad take    **c** Dad is taking
   **b** Dad takes    **d** Is Dad taking

15 In my house, we _____ the internet every day.
   **a** is using    **c** are using
   **b** uses    **d** use

16 It's cold, so we _____ our bikes these days.
   **a** is riding    **c** isn't riding
   **b** riding    **d** aren't riding

17 We've got a _____ cake in the fridge.
   **a** much    **c** lots of
   **b** lot of    **d** many

18 'I'm in the school play this year.'
   'That's great. What role _____?'
   **a** do you play    **c** are you playing
   **b** you are playing    **d** you play

19 '_____ nice clothes to school?'
   'Yes I do, every day.'
   **a** Do you wear    **c** Are you wearing
   **b** You wear    **d** You are wearing

20 Ryan is eating cereal at the _____.
   **a** moment    **c** now
   **b** day    **d** always

# Reading

**A** Read the *Exam Reminder*. In the *Exam Task*, are the first lines of the conversations questions, statements or commands?

_____

**B** Now complete the *Exam Task*.

## Exam Task

Complete the five conversations. Choose **a**, **b** or **c**.

**1** Remember to wear your sweater.
  **a** No, thanks.
  **b** OK, I will.
  **c** It's pretty and warm.

**2** Why don't we play in the garden?
  **a** It's behind the house.
  **b** There are lovely flowers.
  **c** I think it's too cold.

**3** What's your favourite thing to do in winter?
  **a** Let's play in the snow.
  **b** We've got skis.
  **c** I like building snowmen.

**4** Where did you have lunch?
  **a** With my sister Kylie.
  **b** In the kitchen as usual.
  **c** Around 1 p.m.

**5** That's a great snowboard!
  **a** Thanks, it was a gift.
  **b** Yes, you can use it.
  **c** No, it's my brother's.

# Vocabulary

**A** Use the words to make compound nouns and match them to the photos.
Check whether the compound nouns should be one or two words.

animals  bike  board  light  quad  rise  slide  snow  sun  house  water  wild

1 _____

2 _____

3 _____

4 _____

5 _____

6 _____

**B** Circle the correct words.

1 It's going to rain tomorrow, so let's ride / visit a museum.

2 I want to get up early and attend / watch the sunrise.

3 Kelly will take part / go on in a fun run this year.

4 We need to have / walk on the footpath so we don't get lost.

5 We will go / spend all day on the mountain and it will be great fun!

**C** Complete the sentences with the words from B that you didn't circle.

1 Let's _____ a trip to a snow park.

2 They have a concert in the park every summer and we always _____ it.

3 Can you _____ an elephant in a wildlife park?

4 This winter, I want to _____ ice skating!

5 We _____ lots of fun every time we go to the amusement park.

**D** Complete the dialogue with the correct form of *have* or *take*.

**Jake:** Louis, do you want to (1) _____ lunch at my house on Saturday? We're (2) _____ a picnic outside and my mum's going to cook.

**Louis:** That sounds great. What's the best way to get to your house?

**Jake:** You can (3) _____ the bus to Hampshire Street. My address is 37 Hampshire Street.

**Louis:** Great. Shall I bring something?

**Jake:** No, that's OK. We've got lots of food and drink, and we can (4) _____ an ice-cream after lunch. And then we can go to the park. I want to (5) _____ photos there.

**Louis:** Cool! I'd like to (6) _____ a go at that. I'll bring my camera, too.

**Jake:** That sounds like fun. So, see you Saturday!

**E** Read the *Exam Reminder*. Then complete the *Exam Task*.

## Exam Task

Read the sentences about Lily's trip to an amusement park. Choose the best word (**a**, **b** or **c**) for each answer.

1 My friends and I _____ an amusement park on Saturday.
   **a** arrived    **b** attended    **c** visited

2 They all wanted to _____ the big, scary rollercoaster.
   **a** ride    **b** go    **c** have

3 I didn't join them; instead, I got on the Ferris _____.
   **a** slide    **b** ride    **c** wheel

4 I had a great _____, but Ron didn't feel well after snowboarding.
   **a** hour    **b** time    **c** minute

5 Let's _____ turns on the water slide.
   **a** make    **b** have    **c** take

## Exam Reminder

**Using your knowledge of vocabulary**
- Words often go together to form a word group. In some tasks, a word from a word group is often missing.
- Learning word groups helps find the missing word.
- Use word maps to help you learn word groups.

# Grammar

## Past Simple *to be*; Regular & Irregular Forms; Questions & Negatives; *Yes / No* Questions & Short Answers; Time Expressions

**A** Write sentences and questions with these words and the correct form of *to be*.

1 I / at a birthday party / two days ago
_____

2 you / in English class / yesterday / ?
_____

3 who / with you / at the cinema / ?
_____

4 there / not / 12 people / on the trip
_____

5 where / your parents / last night / ?
_____

6 there / not / a place to sit / ?
_____

**B** Complete the sentences with the correct form of these verbs.

buy   drink   go   plan   play   stop   study   take

1 We _____ to a music concert yesterday evening.

2 I _____ history for several hours last weekend.

3 The driver _____ to let Jane out.

4 She _____ her outfit for a very good price.

5 They _____ a trip to Paris with their best friends.

6 He _____ the bus to work the other day.

7 They _____ lots of coffee to wake up.

8 The kids _____ games together all afternoon.

**C** Complete the sentences with the correct form of the words in brackets.

1 I _____ (**not go**) to the amusement park yesterday.

2 Who _____ (**you meet**) at the new hamburger place?

3 _____ (**you / pass**) your exams last week?

4 When _____ (**Michael / get**) to your house?

5 _____ (**Ms Mills / give**) an exam in class yesterday?

6 They _____ (**not see**) us at the supermarket yesterday morning.

7 Why _____ (**you / not call**) me last night?

8 Jim _____ (**not wear**) his new boots to football practice.

**D** Choose the correct answers.

1 'Did you enjoy your friend's play?'    '_____.'
  a  Yes, I was          b  Yes, I did          c  Yes, I enjoyed

2 'Did they bring great music to the party?'    '_____.'
  a  No, they didn't bring    b  Yes, they brought    c  No, they didn't

3 'Did John go snowboarding yesterday?'    '_____.'
  a  Yes, he didn't        b  Yes, he went        c  Yes, he did

4 'When did you buy those sunglasses?'    'It was _____ afternoon.'
  a  yesterday          b  last          c  an

5 'When did Paul and Angela go swimming?'    'I think they went _____ weekend.'
  a  a             b  yesterday          c  last

6 'When was your first day at work?'    'It was four days _____.'
  a  last           b  ago           c  yesterday

**E** Read the *Exam Reminder*. Then complete the *Exam Task*.

## Exam Reminder

**Checking verb tenses & endings**
- Read the text first to understand the general idea.
- Check which gaps need verbs and use the text to help you decide which tense to use.
- Look for the subject in the text so you know what verb ending to use.
- Read the text with your answers to check that they make sense.

## Exam Task

Read Helen's email to her friend about her trip to a new park. Write **ONE** word for each space.

⬤ ◯ ◯                  Email Message

From: Helen
To: Sue

Hi Sue,
How are you? I **(1)** _____ a really
great day yesterday. I **(2)** _____ with
my brother to the new park in our neighbourhood. They
finished it **(3)** _____ week and yesterday
**(4)** _____ the opening day of the park.
There **(5)** _____ lots of people from my
neighbourhood there. The park **(6)** _____
got some really nice rides, such as a slide and a merry-go-
round. My brother went on the slide several times. I think he
really **(7)** _____ it! After, we got some ice-
cream and sat **(8)** _____ a bench to eat
it. A woman **(9)** _____ a photo of us and
she sent it to my smartphone. I **(10)** _____
looking at it now – it's really cool! I think you'd like the park a
lot, so we should go some time.
Bye for now,
Helen

# Listening

**A** Read the *Exam Reminder*. What is similar and what is different about the pictures in the first question of the *Exam Task*?

_____

**B** 🔊 5.1 ▶ Listen and complete the *Exam Task*.

## Exam Task

You will hear five short conversations. You will hear each conversation twice. There is one question for each conversation. For each question, choose the right answer (**a**, **b** or **c**).

**1** Which ride did Annie miss?

a    b    c

**4** Which person is Mary's uncle?

a    b    c

**2** When did Doug study for his science exam?

a    b    c

**5** How much is the bus tour?

a   b   c

**3** What is Rachel's favourite food?

a    b    c

**C** 🔊 5.2 ▶ Listen again and check your answers.

# Writing: a diary

**A** Match the feelings to the statements.

1 We took a tour of London yesterday. ☐
2 I swam in the sea last weekend. ☐
3 We walked in a bad part of town last night. ☐
4 I studied maths for several hours yesterday afternoon. ☐
5 We cooked some fish on our camping trip. ☐
6 I saw a sick bird in the park the other day. ☐

a It tasted great!
b The sights were fantastic.
c It was really sad.
d It was very scary.
e The water was amazing!
f It was very boring.

## B Put the events of this diary entry in the correct order.

**29th April**

Today my sister and I went sightseeing around the village. (1) _____ I bought a chocolate croissant and my sister got a small sandwich. They were very tasty! (2) _____ There were some paintings by local artists. The paintings were lovely. (3) _____ The trees were quite nice and I really enjoyed it. (4) _____ We ran back to the hotel to get dry. It was rather funny! (5) _____The programmes were in French and it was a little boring. My French is not so good! (6) _____.The waiter was really nice and the place was beautiful. The food was good, too! I hope tomorrow is as exciting as today!

a  After that, we walked through a park near the centre.

b  Next, we watched TV for a while in the room.

c  First, we went to a bakery in the town square.

d  Then, it started to rain.

e  Next, we visited a local museum on the other side of the village.

f  Finally, my parents took us to a lovely restaurant.

## C The email below is a response to a friend's email. Read the email and answer the questions.

Write a rough draft on paper first.

Remember to include the answers to the three questions in your email.

Read your draft carefully and make any necessary changes.

Hi Frank,
Thanks for your email. Yesterday I went to an amusement park with friends.
I rode a very big rollercoaster. It was the best! I took lots of photos – I'll send you some!
Bye for now,
Dave

1  How does Dave begin the email?
_____

2  What was Frank's first question to Dave?
_____

3  What was Frank's second question to Dave?
_____

4  What was Frank's third question to Dave?
_____

5  How does Dave describe his feelings about a ride?
_____

6  How does Dave end the email?
_____

## D Read and complete the *Exam Task*. Don't forget to use the *Useful Expressions* on page 67 of your Student's Book.

## Exam Task

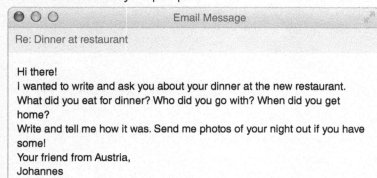

Read the email from your pen pal.

Re: Dinner at restaurant

Hi there!
I wanted to write and ask you about your dinner at the new restaurant.
What did you eat for dinner? Who did you go with? When did you get home?
Write and tell me how it was. Send me photos of your night out if you have some!
Your friend from Austria,
Johannes

Write an email to your pen pal and answer the questions. Write **25–35** words.

➲ Writing Reference p. 174 in Student's Book

# Reading

**A** Read the *Exam Reminder*. Then look at the first line of the *Exam Task*. Without looking at the answers, can you think of a response?

_____

**B** Now complete the *Exam Task*.

## Exam Task

Complete the dialogue between two friends. What does Lewis say to Michelle? Choose the correct answer **A – H**. There are three letters you do not need to use.

**Michelle:** My little sister and I went to a petting zoo last Saturday.

**Lewis:** (1) _____

**Michelle:** It was lots of fun. I love being around such cool, friendly animals.

**Lewis:** (2) _____

**Michelle:** They had donkeys, sheep, goats, rabbits and ponies.

**Lewis:** (3) _____

**Michelle:** They let us feed them, too.

**Lewis:** (4) _____

**Michelle:** No, the zoo gave us some for free. It's safer that way.

**Lewis:** (5) _____

**Michelle:** My mum paid for us, but I don't think it was a lot.

## Exam Reminder

**Reading the completed dialogue**

- Read the dialogue and think about a response to each line before you look at the answer choices. Remember to read the line after the gap as well as the line before.
- Read the whole dialogue after you choose your answers to ensure it makes sense and flows well.

**A** What was your favourite animal?

**B** What kinds of animals were there?

**C** How much did the food cost?

**D** Did you bring food for them?

**E** Oh really? How was it?

**F** How much did it cost to get in?

**G** What did you do on Saturday?

**H** Wow, that's a lot!

# Vocabulary

**A** Match these words to the photos.

| butterfly | claw | feathers | leopard | scales | tail |

1 _____

2 _____

3 _____

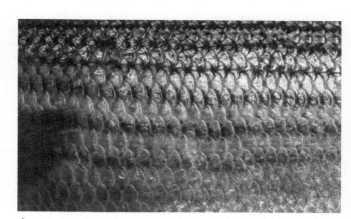

4 _____

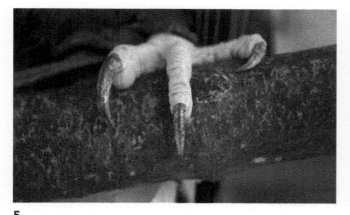

5 _____

6 _____

**B** Match the words to the definitions.

1 This type of animal lives in wet and dry places. ☐    **a** beak
2 A bird uses this to fly. ☐    **b** fin
3 This is a bird's mouth. ☐    **c** fur
4 This is on a fish's body. ☐    **d** wing
5 Snakes belong to this animal family. ☐    **e** reptile
6 This is animal hair. ☐    **f** amphibian

## C Circle the correct words.

1 A(n) bee / ostrich has got a really long neck.
2 There is a small goose / mouse living inside a wall in our house.
3 The cow at my grandparents' farm just gave birth to a monkey / calf.
4 I don't like snakes / tarantulas because they have too many legs.
5 My friend's turtle has got a very hard shell / skin.
6 My parents often ride sheep / horses at the weekends.

## D Complete the blog with these words.

babies   bodies   cute   dangerous   puppies   tiny

○ ○ ○

**20th August**  〉 Topics 〉 Blogs

It was an exciting day in my house yesterday. Our dog Samantha had (1) _____! I can't believe how (2) _____ their faces are. They're also very (3) _____ and they can fit in my hand! That's how small their (4) _____ are. I don't hold them at all because I don't want to upset Samantha. We shouldn't take (5) _____ away from any animal! It's (6) _____ to do that because they can get sick, and their mum can get very angry, too. So, I'll be glad when they get older, so we can play!

## E Read the *Exam Reminder*. Then complete the *Exam Task*.

### Exam Task

Read the descriptions of some words for parts of a body. What is the word for each one? The first letter is already there. There is one space for **each letter** in the word.

1 This is on the outside of our bodies.      s _ _ _
2 You use these to hold a pencil.            f _ _ _ _ _ _
3 We walk with these.                        f _ _ _
4 These are inside our mouths.               t _ _ _ _
5 A bird uses this to eat.                   b _ _ _

# Grammar

## Comparative Adjectives; Making Comparisons; Using Adjectives

### A Write sentences with these words and comparative adjectives.

1 lion / large / tiger

_____

2 bear / heavy / ostrich

_____

3 butterfly / colourful / fly

_____

4 fish / good pet / bird

_____

5 hippopotamus / big / crocodile

_____

6 tarantula / scary pet / reptile

_____

**B** Complete the sentences with these words.

as (x2)   from   like   not   same

1 In my opinion, a spider is _____ scary as a snake.
2 My best friend's dog is _____ as big as my cat!
3 I don't think cheetahs are very different _____ leopards.
4 Our parrot is the _____ as our neighbour's parrot!
5 A dolphin looks _____ a fish, but it's a mammal.
6 A penguin's wings are not _____ long as an eagle's wings.

**C** Complete the questions with one word in each gap.

1 'How _____ is your dog Ralph?'
  'He'll be six in March.'
2 'How _____ is an elephant?'
  'It can run almost 24 kilometres per hour!'
3 'How _____ is a male ostrich?'
  'It can grow as high as three metres!'

4 'How _____ is a python?'
  'It can be almost six metres long!'
5 'How _____ is your pet parrot?'
  'He makes a lot of noise because he's always talking!'
6 'How _____ is your pet lizard?'
  'He can fit in my hand!'

**D** Look at the photos and complete the sentences with the correct form of *look*, *sound* or *feel*.

1 This animal _____ like a tiger, but it's an ocelot.

2 The scales of an iguana _____ very hard and dry.

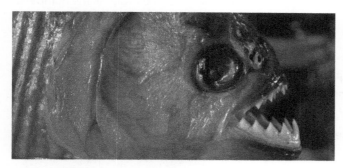

3 Piranha fish are dangerous and they _____ like a dog when they make noise!

4 A sphynx is a cat with no fur. Its skin _____ like soft leather!

5 This is a walrus. A walrus can whistle and it _____ like a bird!

6 Koalas _____ very cute, but they've got sharp claws and can bite!

**E** Read the *Exam Reminder*. Then complete the *Exam Task*.

## Exam Task

Read the descriptions of two kinds of monkeys. Choose the best word (**a**, **b** or **c**) for each space.

### Lemurs and spider monkeys

I visited the city zoo last weekend and I saw some really interesting animals. My favourite animals are monkeys because they look a little bit (**1**) _____ people. They are very different (**2**) _____ us. We're much larger (**3**) _____ them and we haven't got any fur!

The two monkeys I liked the most were the ring-tailed lemur and the spider monkey. They're both quite friendly, but I think the spider monkey is (**4**) _____ as friendly as the lemur. There was an area with lemurs, and you can enter it and sit with them. They run around and jump on you. It's a fantastic experience!

But you can't do that with the spider monkeys. They are (**5**) _____ dangerous than the lemurs. But they are still very cute. The spider monkey has got really long arms and legs. They are much (**6**) _____ than the arms and legs of the lemurs. This is how the spider monkey (**7**) _____ like a spider. Their arms and legs allow them to climb trees (**8**) _____ than a lemur. How fast can you climb a tree? Both lemurs and spider monkeys can do it in seconds. It's amazing to watch!

| | | | | | | | | | | | |
|---|---|---|---|---|---|---|---|---|---|---|---|
| **1** | a | as | b | like | c | than | **5** | a | more | b | like | c | as |
| **2** | a | like | b | as | c | from | **6** | a | long | b | longer | c | more |
| **3** | a | as | b | from | c | than | **7** | a | hears | b | looks | c | sees |
| **4** | a | like | b | not | c | more | **8** | a | faster | b | very | c | fast |

## Exam Reminder

**Reading before & after**

- Read the text before you look at the options to get the general idea first.
- After you choose your answers, go back and read the whole text again to make sure your answers make sense.

# Listening

**A** Read the *Exam Reminder*. What is the question in the *Exam Task*?

_____

## Exam Reminder

**Listening for false information**

- Speakers often give false information and then correct it. Make a note of this while you are listening.
- Remember to underline the question in the task. The answers will be in the same order as the numbers.

**B** 6.1 ▶❚❚ Listen and complete the *Exam Task*.

## Exam Task

Listen to two teenagers talking. Who has got which pet? For questions **1 – 5**, write a letter **A – G** next to each item. You will hear the conversation twice. There are two letters you don't need to use.

| 1 | Paulo | ☐ |
| 2 | Marty | ☐ |
| 3 | Sarah | ☐ |
| 4 | Stan | ☐ |
| 5 | Arnold | ☐ |

**A** painted turtle  **E** canary
**B** rosy boa  **F** gecko
**C** budgie  **G** cockatoo
**D** tarantula

**C** 6.2 ▶❚❚ Listen again and check your answers.

## Learning Reminder

**Writing facts**

- Make sure your facts are correct by checking the information that you write.
- Use the Present Simple for facts. Do not use contractions in formal writing.
- Include facts to explain why something is the way it is. Use *because* to give reasons if necessary.

# Writing: a fact file

**A** Write the contractions in the sentences as full words.

1 My pet is a parrot and she's two years old. _____
2 My pet guinea pig's got brown fur. _____
3 My name is Rachel and I'm a veterinarian. _____
4 We can't give our pets junk food. _____

**B** Read the fact file. Then read the student's text. There are six mistakes. Cross out the mistakes and write the correct information in the spaces.

## Fact File: Parrots

- 372 different types
- Can live over 80 years
- Often brightly coloured
- Have strong legs and sharp claws
- Like warm weather

- Very clever
- Eat seeds and insects
- Can weigh between 0.5 and 4 kg
- Can learn over 1,000 words

Parrots are interesting animals. There are 272 different types of parrots in the world. They can live a long time – around 18 years. They are very colourful and they enjoy cold weather. They are strong, and they eat seeds and vegetables. They can weigh between 4 and 5 kg. Parrots can talk and can learn over 100 words.

1 _____   3 _____   5 _____
2 _____   4 _____   6 _____

**C** Read the texts and circle the correct words in the fact file.

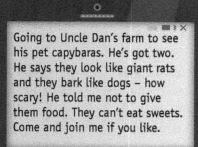

Going to Uncle Dan's farm to see his pet capybaras. He's got two. He says they look like giant rats and they bark like dogs – how scary! He told me not to give them food. They can't eat sweets. Come and join me if you like.

Make sure you check the spelling of information when you complete gaps.

**2nd May** › **Topics** › **Animals**

### Life with a capybara

I wanted to write about my pet capybara. Many people think they are good pets. They're very friendly, but they're a lot of work. They can't live indoors … you need a lot of space. My capybara grew to be 50 centimetres tall and he weighs 60 kilograms. They can only eat grass or special food. Please think carefully before getting one!

Review irregular verbs forms and plural nouns.

## Fact File: Capybara

| | |
|---|---|
| Looks like: | giant (**1**) rat / dog |
| Must live: | (**2**) indoors / outdoors |
| Behaviour: | (**3**) scary / friendly |
| Can't eat: | (**4**) grass / sweets |
| Can weigh: | (**5**) 50 /60 kilograms |
| Easy to care for: | (**6**) yes / no |

**D** Read and complete the *Exam Task*. Don't forget to use the *Useful Expressions* on page 79 of your Student's Book.

Exam Task

Read the email and the webpage. Fill in the information in the Fact File.

Email Message

Re: Looking after my pets

Hi there,
My holiday is coming up soon! Thanks for agreeing to look after my guinea pigs. Joyce and Pippin are excited to meet you! Joyce is the brown one, and Pippin's brown, black and white. I give them fresh spinach and carrots every day, and I change their water every two days. I'll come to your house later to give you my keys.
See you soon,
Jake

### Fact File:

| | |
|---|---|
| Animal: | guinea pig |
| Colours: | brown, white, black and (**1**) _____ |
| Food: | (**2**) _____ |
| Change water: | every (**3**) _____ |
| Behaviour: | – make noises that sound like (**4**) '_____' |
| | – friendly, but can become (**5**) _____ |

Guinea pigs

Guinea pigs are small animals. They are about 10 cm long and weigh 400–600 grams. Their fur can be white, brown, grey and black, and they can be one colour or multi-coloured.

They often make loud noises – it sounds like 'wheek'!

They are friendly pets and they love to have company.

Interesting fact: in Switzerland, you have to keep two guinea pigs as pets. You cannot keep just one, because they can get very lonely!

↪ Writing Reference p. 175 in Student's Book

# Vocabulary

**A**   **Choose the correct answers.**

**1**   Let's go on the water _____.
- **a**   coaster
- **b**   run
- **c**   slide
- **d**   wheel

**2**   At the end of the day, it's nice to _____ a sunset.
- **a**   visit
- **b**   attend
- **c**   watch
- **d**   have

**3**   Beth decided to _____ a go at snowboarding.
- **a**   make
- **b**   do
- **c**   have
- **d**   take

**4**   Are there many animals at the _____?
- **a**   waterpark
- **b**   snow park
- **c**   amusement park
- **d**   wildlife park

**5**   I can't wait to go _____ on the mountain this winter.
- **a**   riding
- **b**   skiing
- **c**   swimming
- **d**   surfing

**6**   My parents are taking _____ in a 10 km run this year.
- **a**   part
- **b**   place
- **c**   care
- **d**   time

**7**   Be careful – that animal's got very sharp _____.
- **a**   wings
- **b**   shells
- **c**   feet
- **d**   teeth

**8**   The bird's _____ were green, yellow and blue.
- **a**   fins
- **b**   scales
- **c**   feathers
- **d**   beaks

**9**   What do the _____ of a fish feel like?
- **a**   claws
- **b**   tails
- **c**   fingers
- **d**   scales

**10**   The giant panda is one of the most well-known _____ species in the world.
- **a**   prey
- **b**   endangered
- **c**   camouflaged
- **d**   poisonous

**11**   Dogs, cats, horses and pigs are all _____.
- **a**   mammals
- **b**   birds
- **c**   amphibians
- **d**   reptiles

**12**   We saw a very heavy _____ at the zoo.
- **a**   tadpole
- **b**   rhinoceros
- **c**   butterfly
- **d**   tarantula

**13**   My aunt's cow had a baby _____ the other day.
- **a**   chick
- **b**   calf
- **c**   puppy
- **d**   kitten

**14**   A _____ is a type of cat and it can run very fast.
- **a**   leopard
- **b**   monkey
- **c**   snake
- **d**   dolphin

**15**   I _____ a rollercoaster for the first time yesterday.
- **a**   had
- **b**   did
- **c**   took
- **d**   rode

**16**   We can _____ turns playing this game if you like.
- **a**   take
- **b**   make
- **c**   do
- **d**   play

**17**   Let's _____ a picnic in the park if the weather's nice.
- **a**   go
- **b**   take
- **c**   have
- **d**   do

**18**   My sister and I are doing a fun _____ next month.
- **a**   ride
- **b**   path
- **c**   walk
- **d**   run

**19**   How much time did you _____ at the amusement park?
- **a**   pass
- **b**   do
- **c**   spend
- **d**   take

**20**   I love my cat's _____ … it feels so soft!
- **a**   shell
- **b**   claw
- **c**   skin
- **d**   fur

# Grammar

**B** **Choose the correct answers.**

1 'Where _____ you yesterday, Kevin?'
   'I was at home. I wasn't feeling well.'
   
   a  are              c  was
   b  is               d  were

2 Jill _____ a loud noise outside her room the other day.
   
   a  hearing          c  hears
   b  heard            d  hear

3 'Why _____ you his smartphone?'
   'He got a new one.'
   
   a  Tom gave         c  did Tom give
   b  Tom gives        d  does Tom give

4 Danielle and Kip _____ at the party yesterday evening.
   
   a  isn't            c  aren't
   b  wasn't           d  weren't

5 'Did you see your grandparents over the summer?'
   'Yes, _____.'
   
   a  they did         c  I saw
   b  I did            d  they saw

6 Wendy read a book for three hours _____ night.
   
   a  a                c  last
   b  yesterday        d  ago

7 A budgie is _____ than a parrot.
   
   a  more small       c  small
   b  smaller          d  small more

8 'Snakes are scary pets.'
   'Yes, they're _____ than tarantulas.
   
   a  more worse       c  bad
   b  more bad         d  worse

9 'Which is bigger, a zebra or a horse?'
   'I think horses are bigger _____ zebras.'
   
   a  to               c  as
   b  from             d  than

10 'Do you like my pet goat?'
   'Yes, it looks _____ a nice animal.'
   
   a  as               c  –
   b  so               d  like

11 'Can you hear my pet hamster?'
   'Yes, it _____ like a bird!'
   
   a  looks            c  sounds
   b  hears            d  feels

12 Fish are different _____ reptiles because they breathe water.
   
   a  from             c  not
   b  as               d  than

13 'When did you talk to Henry?'
   'I talked to him four days _____.'
   
   a  ago              c  yesterday
   b  last             d  from

14 House cats in North America are _____ same as house cats in Europe.
   
   a  like             c  the
   b  so               d  as

15 'Did you touch the tarantula?'
   'Yes, it felt _____ furry!'
   
   a  as               c  like
   b  not              d  –

16 An elephant is _____ as tall as a giraffe.
   
   a  –                c  so
   b  like             d  not

17 Georgina _____ the photos because her internet connection stopped working.
   
   a  sends            c  didn't send
   b  sent             d  doesn't send

18 'What did you do on Sunday?'
   'I _____ anything.'
   
   a  don't do         c  didn't
   b  didn't do        d  did

19 'Were your friends at the dance?'
   'No, _____.'
   
   a  they didn't      c  they don't
   b  they aren't      d  they weren't

20 'When was the exam?'
   'It was _____.'
   
   a  yesterday        c  night
   b  a week           d  two days

## Reading

**A** Read the *Exam Reminder*. What will be true about an *Exam Task* question if you choose the answer 'Doesn't say'?

_____

**B** Now complete the *Exam Task*.

# Dream Inventions

Inventions sometimes come from dreams. The famous director Christopher Nolan filmed *Inception* in 2010, but he wrote the script from a dream he had in 2002. The film's characters enter each other's dreams. They share experiences and they can change each other's lives through dreams. Film fans really liked the idea and Nolan's film was the most popular film that year.

In science, we use a table to put elements like oxygen and carbon in order. We call it the periodic table of elements. Before this table existed, Dmitri Mendeleev, a Russian scientist, saw it in a dream. He woke up straight away and wrote it down. He only made one correction later on. Otherwise, it was perfect! At the time, scientists only knew of 56 elements. Today they have discovered almost 120 elements, all present in Mendeleev's table.

American inventor Elias Howe dreamt of a better sewing machine. In his dream, he was building one for a terrible king in a faraway land. The king gave him 24 hours to build the machine … or die! Howe woke up at 4 a.m. and started making a new type of needle. It was a success! Today, needles have 'eyes' in them because of Howe's dream, or at least that's how the story goes.

Read the article about inventions. Are sentences **1 – 7** 'Right' (**A**) or 'Wrong' (**B**)? If there is not enough information to answer 'Right' (**A**) or 'Wrong' (**B**), choose 'Doesn't say' (**C**).

1 Nolan made his film when he dreamt of it. ☐

2 Many people loved the film's story. ☐

3 Mendeleev wrote his periodic table at 4 a.m. ☐

4 His table had fewer elements than the table today. ☐

5 Howe dreamt about building a machine for a king he knew in real life. ☐

6 He invented many sewing machines in his life. ☐

7 Howe's needle worked very well. ☐

# Vocabulary

**A Match the first parts of the questions 1–6 to the second parts a–f.**

1 Did you remember to switch ☐

2 When you have a chance, can you look ☐

3 Is there a place to plug ☐

4 Can you turn ☐

5 Is it OK to wear ☐

6 Do you have to pull ☐

a earphones at your job?

b at this message on the computer?

c in a phone charger in this room?

d on the lights so we can see better?

e this handle to open the car boot?

f off your mobile during the exam?

**B Complete the words for the definitions.**

1 You use this to open a door.  d _ _ _   h _ _ _ _ _

2 You can talk on this and use the internet.  s _ _ _ _ _ _ _ _ _

3 This turns on things from far away.  r _ _ _ _ _   c _ _ _ _ _ _

4 You look at this to read things on the internet.  c _ _ _ _ _ _ _   s _ _ _ _ _

5 You have one of these to get clean.  s _ _ _ _ _

6 You can listen to music on this.  r _ _ _ _

**C Complete the sentences with these words.**

cooker   fridge   knife   oven   table   washing machine

1 Sarah put the cake in the _____ to cook for 45 minutes.

2 You can use this _____ to cut the vegetables.

3 My clothes are in the _____; they'll be clean soon.

4 Please pass me the plates. They are on the _____.

5 Can you get the milk out of the _____?

6 You can use the _____ to boil the potatoes.

**D** Choose the correct answers.

1 Jane made a _____ table for her living room.
   a wooden, small, round
   b round, small, wooden
   c small, round, wooden

2 Did you buy that _____ dress we saw yesterday?
   a white, long, cotton
   b long, white, cotton
   c cotton, long, white

3 We can put the spaghetti in that _____ bowl.
   a big, red, plastic
   b red, plastic, big
   c plastic, red, big

4 They sat at a _____ desk during the interview.
   a metal, black, rectangular
   b black, rectangular, metal
   c rectangular, black, metal

5 They decorated the tree with several _____ ornaments.
   a glass, blue, little
   b little, blue, glass
   c blue, glass, little

6 Tom cut his finger on a _____ object.
   a sharp, brown, tiny
   b tiny, brown, sharp
   c tiny, sharp, brown

**E** Circle the correct words.

Do you wonder what life was like before electronics? How did people keep their food (**1**) warm / cold without a fridge? How did they clean their (**2**) house / clothes without a washing machine? It seems like life would be very difficult without these things, or even dangerous. For example, they didn't have (**3**) electric ovens / phone chargers a hundred years ago, so they probably cooked food using a wood fire. I guess it was quite dangerous, but at least they were able to make a hot meal. They didn't have any (**4**) lights / showers, either, so they had to use candles to see in the rooms at night. And how did they get news without a radio to (**5**) read / listen to or a television to (**6**) hear / watch? I think I prefer life today, to be honest!

# Grammar

### Superlative Adjectives; *The one, The ones* …; Expressing Purpose; *Will* for predictions

**A** Complete the sentences with the superlative forms of the adjectives in brackets.

1 Jacob is the _____ (**tall**) student in my class.

2 I think dogs are the _____ (**friendly**) pets!

3 Smartphones are the _____ (**good**) type of phones.

4 A robot car seems like the _____ (**scary**) way to travel.

5 Dan bought the _____ (**expensive**) computer in the shop.

6 Microwave ovens are the _____ (**bad**) devices for cooking food.

7 That shopping centre is the _____ (**far**) from our house.

8 That company makes the _____ (**thin**) laptops.

9 The sun is the _____ (**beautiful**) star in the sky.

10 My sister Diane is the _____ (**fit**) person in my family.

**B** Complete the sentences with *one* or *ones*.

1 These devices are the _____ that we bought today.

2 These awards are mine. I'm most proud of the _____ from the maths competition.

3 These books are the _____ from the school library.

4 These offices belong to the inventors. Mr White's office is the _____ on the right.

5 This computer is faster than the _____ I have on my desk at home.

6 These sandwiches are for the kids. The _____ on that tray have tomato and ham.

**C** Complete the sentences with the correct form of the verb in brackets.

1 This device is used to _____ (**clean**) the computer keyboard.

2 I use this light for _____ (**read**) in bed at night.

3 This room is used for _____ (**do**) the laundry.

4 These buttons are used to _____ (**move**) the robot's arms.

5 A thermometer is used for _____ (**tell**) the temperature.

6 We can use these night goggles for _____ (**see**) things at night.

**D** Write sentences with these words and *will* or *won't*.

1 a spaceship / travel / another solar system

_____

2 humans / be able / walk / on the sun

_____

3 robots / help / teachers / in the classroom

_____

4 our pets / clean / our homes

_____

5 trains / travel / through the earth's centre

_____

6 mankind / end / world hunger

_____

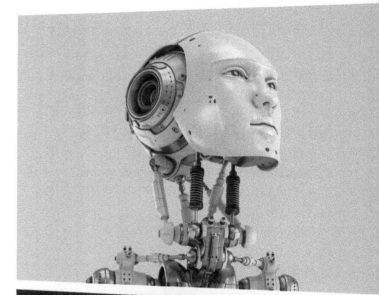

**E** Circle the correct words.

**Robbie:** Marsha, do you think people will live on other planets one day?

**Marsha:** Yes, they (**1**) won't / will. There are many planets in the sky and scientists find new planets every day. The planets similar to earth are the (**2**) one / ones we can probably live on.

**Robbie:** I know that scientists have special telescopes. They are used for (**3**) find / finding new planets. Maybe they will find a planet in a solar system near us. That's the (**4**) one / ones we'll send a spaceship to. It'll probably be a long time from now.

**Marsha:** Well, it makes sense to visit the (**5**) close / closest planet with life. I think that will be the (**6**) exciting / most exciting news!

# Listening

**A** Read the *Exam Reminder*. For which gaps in the *Exam Task* will spelling be very important?

_____

**B** 🔊 **7.1** Listen and complete the *Exam Task*.

## Exam Task

You will hear a man looking for a new phone charger. Listen and complete each question. You will hear the conversation twice.

**New phone charger**

Name of man's phone: **(1)** _____ P10 Lite

Arrives at shop: in **(2)** _____ days

Price: **(3)** £ _____

Shop address: 241 **(4)** _____ Road

Closes on Saturday: at **(5)** _____

### Exam Reminder

**Spelling correctly**

- Sometimes speakers spell out a word in a conversation.
- Write the word as you hear the letters. Then check your answer when you listen again.
- Remember to always read through all your answers to check the spelling is correct.

**C** 🔊 **7.2** Listen again and check your answers.

# Writing: captions

**A** Match the captions to the inventions.

### Learning Reminder

**Adding information in captions**

- Captions are short bits of text that go with a photo or illustration. They help readers understand what they're looking at.
- When people take selfies, they write a caption and put the photo and the caption together on social media.

1 ☐

3 ☐

2 ☐

4 ☐

**a** People used washboards to clean their clothes before we had washing machines.

**b** These high-speed passenger trains are the fastest trains in the world.

**c** The abacus is the oldest type of counting machine.

**d** Solar energy powers the light for this pedestrian crossing.

**B** Look at the photo and complete the captions with these words.

| helmet | inventor | old town | platform | speeds | tour |

1 Segways are popular for going on a(n) _____ of a city.
2 This couple is exploring the city's _____ on a pair of Segways.
3 Segways are safe, but it's a good idea to wear a(n) _____.
4 You stand on the Segway's central _____ while you move.
5 The Segway can travel at _____ of up to 20 kilometres per hour.
6 Dean Kamen, the _____ of the Segway, launched it in 2001.

**C** Use the student's notes to complete the form.

There is usually not much space, so write a clear message in just a few words.

Why do you want to attend the robot exhibition? (no more than 25 words)
(1) _____
_____
_____

Forms often ask for more information than just a name, address and number.

Describe an interesting robot you once saw. (no more than 25 words)
(2) _____
_____
_____

robots are very interesting, can learn a lot from them, once saw one that looked like a puppy, moved around like one, had electronic bark, was quite cool

Write a rough draft first to help improve your message.

**D** Read and complete the *Exam Task*. Don't forget to use the *Useful Expressions* on page 93 of your Student's Book.

Exam Task

Read the school flyer and the email. Fill in the information on Gary's permission form.

**School trip – Robot Exhibition**

**Attention all students:**

There will be school trips in April to see the Robot Exhibition at the London Science Museum.

All those interested in attending need to submit their forms by the 19th of March.

There will be two groups going to the exhibition – the first on the weekend of the 22nd of April and the second on the weekend of the 29th of April. Please state on your forms which trip you will attend.

○ ○ ○     Email Message

From: Neil Fox <nfox@ymail.com>
To: Gary Loch <gloch@ymail.com>

Hi Gary,
I'm excited about the school trip in April. I hear there are some really cool robots in this exhibition. You're going to come, aren't you? I hope so! I just wanted to say that my brother's big football match is on the 22nd, so it would be better to go the following weekend, if that's OK with you.
Bye for now,
Neil

**School Trip Permission Form**
Name: (**1**) _____
Name of trip: (**2**) _____
Location: (**3**) _____
Date of trip: (**4**) _____
Contact email: (**5**) _____

↻ Writing Reference p. 176 in Student's Book

## Reading

**A** Read the *Exam Reminder*. What are the subjects of the questions in the *Exam Task*?

_____

**B** Now complete the *Exam Task*.

## Exam Task

Complete the five conversations. Choose **a**, **b** or **c**.

**1** Is this your board game?
  a You can go first.
  b It's my first time.
  c Yes, it's mine.

**2** I want to play outside.
  a That's a good idea.
  b Let's go to my room.
  c I like card games, too.

**3** Where's Nancy?
  a We're classmates.
  b Yes, that's her.
  c She's on her way.

**4** We won the game!
  a It's your turn.
  b You did well!
  c Let's start then.

**5** What does this button do?
  a It makes the player run.
  b Let's go for a ride.
  c That's not mine.

# Vocabulary

**A** **Complete the words in these sentences.**

1  You have to s _ _ _ the wheel to play this game.
2  We need to s _ _ _ _ _ _ the cards first before we start.
3  It's not fair to c _ _ _ _ during a game!
4  Do you know how to d _ _ _ the cards? Give seven cards to each player.
5  My brother is very c _ _ _ _ _ _ _ _ _ _ . He always wants to win every game he plays.
6  You s _ _ _ _ one point when you get the answer right.

**B** **Complete the sentences with the correct form of *lose* or *miss*.**

1  Michael _____ school the other day because he wasn't feeling well.
2  Tom's team _____ the football match on Sunday, 0–2.
3  My best friend moved to a new town and I really _____ him.
4  I can't find the controller … I think I _____ it.
5  Martin was late for work and he _____ an important meeting.
6  Uh, oh … you landed on a bad square. You _____ a turn!
7  I'm trying to hit the ball with the bat, but I'm _____ it again and again!
8  Hurry and get to the station before you _____ the train!

**C** **Write the numbers as words.**

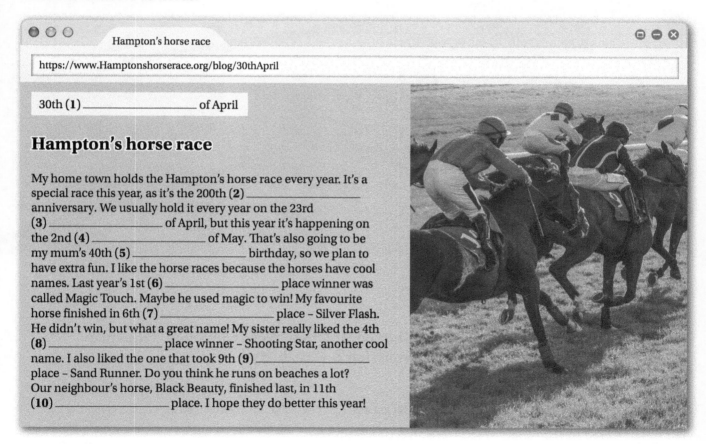

Hampton's horse race

https://www.Hamptonshorserace.org/blog/30thApril

30th **(1)** _____ of April

## Hampton's horse race

My home town holds the Hampton's horse race every year. It's a special race this year, as it's the 200th **(2)** _____ anniversary. We usually hold it every year on the 23rd **(3)** _____ of April, but this year it's happening on the 2nd **(4)** _____ of May. That's also going to be my mum's 40th **(5)** _____ birthday, so we plan to have extra fun. I like the horse races because the horses have cool names. Last year's 1st **(6)** _____ place winner was called Magic Touch. Maybe he used magic to win! My favourite horse finished in 6th **(7)** _____ place – Silver Flash. He didn't win, but what a great name! My sister really liked the 4th **(8)** _____ place winner – Shooting Star, another cool name. I also liked the one that took 9th **(9)** _____ place – Sand Runner. Do you think he runs on beaches a lot? Our neighbour's horse, Black Beauty, finished last, in 11th **(10)** _____ place. I hope they do better this year!

**D** **Circle the correct words.**

1  Shall / Why we play another round of cards?
2  What about playing / going a board game?
3  That feels / sounds like a lot of fun.
4  Why / Shall don't we invite the neighbours to play?
5  I can't believe I went / came last!
6  I don't like this card … can you deal / roll me another?

**E** **Complete the dialogue with these words.**

card  counter  dice  game  score  turn

**Greg:** So, how do you play this board game, Mandy?

**Mandy:** First, you roll the (1) _____ and it gives you a number.

**Greg:** OK. Here I go … oh, I got six. So, I move my (2) _____ six spaces, yeah?

**Mandy:** Right … so, the space you landed on says to take a (3) _____ from the deck.

**Greg:** OK … oh, hmm. My card says that I miss a (4) _____. I guess you get to go now.

**Mandy:** Yes, let's see … I got five! The square says I get ten points. So, we keep the (5) _____ on this piece of paper.

**Greg:** Ten points … wow, you're going to win the (6) _____ before I score anything!

**Mandy:** Don't give up. There are plenty of points for you!

# Grammar

## Zero Conditional; Adverbs To Show Sequence; Other Words To Show Sequence; Modals of Obligation; Modals for Permission & Possibility

**A** **Choose the correct answers.**

1  We clean up the house _____ all the guests leave.
   a  until          b  as soon as

2  I tried several times, but _____ I gave up!
   a  eventually     b  until

3  My dog Lucy eats _____ she's really full!
   a  until          b  in the end

4  She ran very fast, so _____ Lisa won the race.
   a  in the end     b  eventually

5  I became very angry _____ I learnt that Paul cheated!
   a  until          b  as soon as

6  We keep playing the game _____ there's only one person left.
   a  eventually     b  until

**B** **Complete the sentences with the correct form of the verbs in brackets.**

1 After _____ (**play**) for hours, the girls usually go to bed.

2 Before she _____ (**leave**) for school, she has a piece of toast.

3 He plays video games while _____ (**chat**) with friends online.

4 Before _____ (**cross**) the street, Tom always looks for cars.

5 Damien goes to piano lessons after he _____ (**finish**) school.

6 While she _____ (**shuffle**) the cards, Fran explains the rules.

**C** **Write sentences with the zero conditional form of these words.**

1 it / rain / ground / become / wet
If _____

2 you / turn / five / you / start school
When _____

3 we / get hungry / we / not eat
_____ if _____

4 water / freeze / it / go / below 0 degrees
_____ when _____

5 the bell / ring / at 4 p.m. / school / end
When _____

6 you / lose / you / not get / the right answer
_____ if _____

**D** **Circle the correct words.**

1 You must / don't have to be at school at seven. Class starts at eight.

2 You have to / mustn't speak during the exam. It's got a speaking section.

3 We don't have to / mustn't be loud. Grandpa's sleeping.

4 You can / can't go to the shop right now. It's not open yet.

5 She doesn't have to / must attend the show. She's performing in it!

6 They can / can't eat in the garden. It's rather nice outside.

7 We don't have to / can't walk to school. Sean's mum is driving us.

8 You can / must go over to Beth's house if you like.

**E** **Choose the correct answers.**

```
○○○                    Email Message                    ⤢
```
To: Bob, Nancy, Jeffrey
From: Carl
Re: Game night

Hi guys,
I'm excited about game night at my house this Saturday! I'm glad you (1) _____ all
come. You (2) _____ bring anything. My mum's going to cook for us.
My mum's also got a surprise. (3) _____ you win the game, you get a cool prize!
I attached a photo of it – can you tell what it is? So this time, it's really important to
keep the score while (4) _____. We (5) _____ forget to write it down like we did
last time.
So, I can't wait (6) _____ it's Saturday. We're going to have a lot of fun!
See you then,
Carl

| | | | | | |
|---|---|---|---|---|---|
| 1 | **a** can | **b** don't have to | **c** must | | |
| 2 | **a** can't | **b** can | **c** don't have to | | |
| 3 | **a** When | **b** In the end | **c** If | | |
| 4 | **a** plays | **b** playing | **c** play | | |
| 5 | **a** don't have to | **b** must | **c** mustn't | | |
| 6 | **a** until | **b** as soon as | **c** eventually | | |

# Listening

**A** Read the *Exam Reminder*. For which questions in the *Exam Task* will you listen for numbers?

_____

**B** 〔8.1〕 Listen and complete the *Exam Task*.

## Exam Task

Listen to Becky and Laura talking about Laura's game night. For each question, choose the right answer (**a, b** or **c**). You will hear the conversation twice.

**1** How many dice are in the game Laura played?
  **a** two
  **b** six
  **c** ten

**2** How do you win the game?
  **a** build a café
  **b** build a room
  **c** build a hotel

**3** How many people played the game?
  **a** four
  **b** six
  **c** seven

**4** Where did Ben and Nancy go?
  **a** to another game night
  **b** to see Ben's sister in a play
  **c** to see Nancy's sister in a play

**5** Where did Jeff come in the game?
  **a** second
  **b** third
  **c** last

**C** 〔8.2〕 Listen again and check your answers.

# Writing: instructions

**A** Complete the instructions with the correct form of these verbs.

| begin | choose | draw | guess | look | not guess |
|---|---|---|---|---|---|

**1** To play *Pictionary*, first you _____ a card from the deck.

**2** After _____ at the card, you set the timer for 90 seconds.

**3** Before you _____ the round, you turn the timer on.

**4** While _____ the picture, your team tries to guess.

**5** If your team _____ the right answer in time, you win a point.

**6** You lose your turn if your team _____ correctly.

## B Choose the correct answers.

To play musical chairs, **(1)** _____ you arrange chairs in a circle. The backs of the chairs must be on the inside of the circle. **(2)** _____, make sure there is one fewer chair than there are players. If there are eight players, you **(3)** _____ only have seven chairs. **(4)** _____ playing the music, tell everyone to get in a circle around the chairs. Explain that **(5)** _____ the music starts, they start walking in a clockwise manner. When the music stops, they **(6)** _____ find a chair. The player who doesn't get a chair loses and has to miss the next round. **(7)** _____, start the music and play it for a minute or two. Stop the music and watch players run to the chairs! It's great fun! For the next round, remove one chair and continue **(8)** _____ there's only one player left. That's the winner!

| | a | | b | | c | |
|---|---|---|---|---|---|---|
| 1 | a | before | b | first | c | while |
| 2 | a | After | b | At first | c | Next |
| 3 | a | don't have to | b | must | c | mustn't |
| 4 | a | After | b | Before | c | Afterwards |
| 5 | a | after | b | until | c | while |
| 6 | a | mustn't | b | have to | c | don't have to |
| 7 | a | Eventually | b | While | c | Finally |
| 8 | a | before | b | until | c | after |

## C Read the email and the reply. Then circle the correct words.

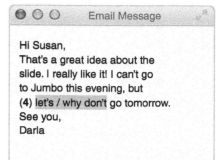

Learn different ways of making suggestions.

Watch your verb forms in suggestions.

Email Message

Hi Darla,
I've got some suggestions for outdoor games. Why don't **(1)** buy / we buy a small water slide for the garden? My mum can help us set it up. Let's **(2)** go / us go to Jumbo later this evening to see what they've got. For food, how about **(3)** get / getting some pizzas?
Susan

Email Message

Hi Susan,
That's a great idea about the slide. I really like it! I can't go to Jumbo this evening, but **(4)** let's / why don't go tomorrow. See you,
Darla

Learn different ways of responding to suggestions.

## D Read and complete the *Exam Task*. Don't forget to use the *Useful Expressions* on page 105 of your Student's Book.

## Exam Task

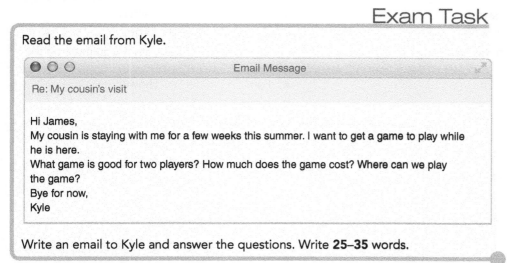

Read the email from Kyle.

Email Message

Re: My cousin's visit

Hi James,
My cousin is staying with me for a few weeks this summer. I want to get a game to play while he is here.
What game is good for two players? How much does the game cost? Where can we play the game?
Bye for now,
Kyle

Write an email to Kyle and answer the questions. Write **25–35** words.

↻ Writing Reference p. 173 in Student's Book

# Vocabulary

**A** Choose the correct answers.

**1** Can I plug _____ my phone charger here?

  **a** out       **c** on

  **b** up        **d** in

**2** We've got a _____, brown, wooden table in our kitchen.

  **a** glass     **c** big

  **b** oval      **d** black

**3** I can't find the remote _____ for the television.

  **a** screen    **c** device

  **b** handle    **d** control

**4** We're in the cinema – switch _____ your phone!

  **a** off       **c** in

  **b** on       **d** out

**5** She put the grapes in a small, _____, plastic bowl.

  **a** short     **c** round

  **b** glass     **d** little

**6** You _____ a wheel to play this game.

  **a** spin      **c** deal

  **b** roll      **d** move

**7** She kicked the ball at the goal, but she _____ it.

  **a** did       **c** lost

  **b** made    **d** missed

**8** I _____ my notebook and I have to get another one.

  **a** lost      **c** gave

  **b** kept     **d** missed

**9** We _____ the cards and then we place them in the centre.

  **a** miss     **c** turn

  **b** shuffle   **d** keep

**10** Can you turn _____ the TV? I want to watch the news.

  **a** on       **c** in

  **b** to       **d** over

**11** Michael _____. That's not fair!

  **a** pressed   **c** cheated

  **b** laughed   **d** drew

**12** We use this large, turquoise, _____ object to put flowers in.

  **a** enormous   **c** glass

  **b** rectangular  **d** purple

**13** How often do you _____ at websites during the day?

  **a** watch    **c** see

  **b** view     **d** look

**14** She called her friend on her _____.

  **a** phone charger  **c** computer screen

  **b** earphone     **d** smartphone

**15** You have to _____ the dice to move forward.

  **a** spin      **c** roll

  **b** jump     **d** shuffle

**16** Who _____ first in the game?

  **a** entered   **c** came

  **b** placed    **d** arrived

**17** Drinking a glass of water can help stop _____.

  **a** earthquakes  **c** predators

  **b** hiccups     **d** fireworks

**18** Jake _____ a day of school because he felt sick.

  **a** lost      **c** missed

  **b** dropped   **d** forgot

**19** I'm listening to my favourite programme on the _____.

  **a** light     **c** shower

  **b** radio     **d** oven

**20** I don't know who won. I didn't _____ the score.

  **a** press     **c** put

  **b** draw     **d** keep

# Grammar

**B** **Choose the correct answers.**

1  Jupiter is _____ planet in our solar system.

   **a**  the largest    **c**  largest

   **b**  the large    **d**  large

2  These shoes are _____ shoes in the shop.

   **a**  the most    **c**  the most expensive

   **b**  most expensive    **d**  expensive

3  'What did you think of the film?'
'That was the _____ film of the year!'

   **a**  worse    **c**  worse than

   **b**  worst    **d**  bad

4  An oven is the _____ way to heat up your food.

   **a**  better than    **c**  best

   **b**  better    **d**  good

5  These clothes are _____ I wore to the ceremony.

   **a**  the one    **c**  ones

   **b**  the ones    **d**  one

6  'What do you use this device for?'
'We use it _____ pasta.'

   **a**  to making    **c**  for make

   **b**  making    **d**  for making

7  If you land on this square, you _____ a turn.

   **a**  not miss    **c**  missed

   **b**  missing    **d**  miss

8  I play chess with my uncle _____ I see him.

   **a**  soon    **c**  when

   **b**  as    **d**  where

9  Before _____ the room, Michael took a deep breath.

   **a**  entered    **c**  enter

   **b**  is entering    **d**  entering

10  'I'm getting a bit hungry.'
'We'll have lunch _____ the food is ready.'

   **a**  eventually    **c**  as soon as

   **b**  in the end    **d**  until

11  You _____ go to the match if you're not feeling well.

   **a**  have to    **c**  must

   **b**  can    **d**  don't have to

12  After they _____, we cleaned up the kitchen.

   **a**  leave    **c**  leaving

   **b**  were leaving    **d**  left

13  'What are the rules of this game?'
'You have to run while _____ an egg on a spoon.'

   **a**  held    **c**  hold

   **b**  to hold    **d**  holding

14  We _____ switch off our phones during the exam.

   **a**  can't    **c**  must

   **b**  mustn't    **d**  can

15  We _____ robots in our kitchens one day.

   **a**  will have    **c**  have

   **b**  had    **d**  are having

16  'Where were you last week?'
'I _____ go to the school play.'

   **a**  mustn't    **c**  must

   **b**  have to    **d**  had to

17  This tree is the most _____ tree in the forest.

   **a**  greatest    **c**  beautiful

   **b**  biggest    **d**  tallest

18  You _____ park your car here. It's not permitted.

   **a**  must    **c**  don't have to

   **b**  can    **d**  mustn't

19  'What is this button for?'
'It's used _____ on the light in the wardrobe.'

   **a**  turning    **c**  to turn

   **b**  for turn    **d**  to turning

20  'These laptops are quite nice.'
'I really like _____ with the big screen.'

   **a**  ones    **c**  the one

   **b**  one    **d**  the ones

## Reading

**A** Read the *Exam Reminder*. What should you do with the options you don't choose in the *Exam Task*?

_____

**B** Now complete the *Exam Task*.

**1**

### Youngest *Olympian* ever

For some Olympic sports, you have to be a certain age. For example, in gymnastics, you have to be at least 16 years old. In boxing, you can't be more than 40 years old. In the 2016 Rio Olympics, the youngest athlete was swimmer Guarika Singh from Nepal. She was 13 years old when she competed in the 100-metre backstroke. So, who is the youngest Olympian ever? That honour goes to Greek athlete Dimitrios Loundras. He won a bronze medal in the 1896 Athens Olympics ... at the age of ten!

**2**

### paragliding lessons

**Learn to paraglide at Falcon Paragliding!**

We've got one-day and two-day courses for beginners. You begin your lessons by getting to know the equipment, what everything is and what it does. Then, an instructor helps you practise on the ground. When you're ready, it's time for your first flight ... all by yourself! Don't worry – students get a radio to use in case of trouble.

Call 00892913 to learn about special offers.

**3**

### Annual Hot-Air Balloon Festival

On the 2nd of June, it's time for Stanford's 16th annual Hot-Air Balloon Festival. Watch over 100 hot-air balloons float in the sky! We're awarding prizes for the most interesting balloons. Other events include the marker drop contest and the 'X marks the spot' landing competition. To enter your balloon, email reservations@stanfordhotair.com.

**4**

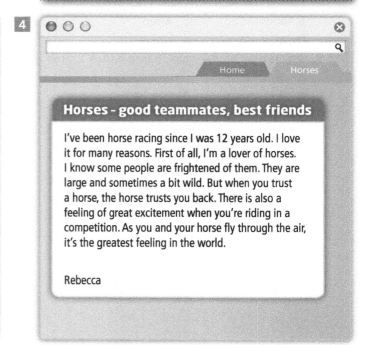

**Horses - good teammates, best friends**

I've been horse racing since I was 12 years old. I love it for many reasons. First of all, I'm a lover of horses. I know some people are frightened of them. They are large and sometimes a bit wild. But when you trust a horse, the horse trusts you back. There is also a feeling of great excitement when you're riding in a competition. As you and your horse fly through the air, it's the greatest feeling in the world.

Rebecca

Read the texts about the four sporting events. For questions **1 – 7**, circle the correct letter **a**, **b** or **c**.

**1** How old do Olympic gymnasts have to be?
   **a** ten             **b** 13             **c** 16

**2** What did Loundras do at the Olympics?
   **a** boxed           **b** won a medal      **c** swam

**3** What do you do first in the paragliding lessons?
   **a** get to know your instructor    **b** learn about the equipment   **c** practise on the ground

**4** Why do paragliding students get a radio?
   **a** for music          **b** to call for help      **c** for a special offer

**5** How many competitions will there be at the Stanford Hot-Air Balloon Festival?
   **a** two            **b** three         **c** four

**6** Why should you contact the balloon festival?
   **a** to reserve a seat      **b** to get information    **c** to enter your balloon

**7** What does Rebecca think of horses?
   **a** They can be frightening to some.    **b** They're very wild.     **c** You shouldn't trust them.

# Vocabulary

**A** **Match these words to the photos.**

goggles   helmet   ice axe   mask   sticks   wetsuit

**1** _____

**2** _____

**3** _____

**4** _____

**5** _____

**6** _____

**B** Match the sports to the equipment.

1. helmet and a parachute ☐
2. crampons, ropes, a helmet, an ice axe ☐
3. a mask, flippers and a wetsuit ☐
4. a board and a wetsuit ☐
5. goggles and sticks ☐
6. knee pads, elbow pads, a helmet and a board ☐

a skiing
b skydiving
c skateboarding
d ice climbing
e scuba diving
f surfing

**C** Complete the sentences with these prepositions.

down   into   off   out of   over   up

1. It was a hot day today and I was glad to jump _____ the pool.
2. There are some stairs over there, so we don't have to jump _____.
3. The cat scared me very badly when it jumped _____ the box.
4. She and her horse jumped _____ the tree branch in the road.
5. My kite is stuck in the tree, but I can't reach it. Can you jump _____ and get it for me?
6. This cliff is dangerous, so whatever you do, don't jump _____ it!

**D** Circle the correct words.

Email Message

Hi Jan,

I wanted to tell you about my (**1**) frightened / frightening sky diving adventure. I can't believe I actually did it! I was with my dad and another group of guys. My dad and I jumped (**2**) out of / onto the plane together. It was funny because right before we jumped, he told me I was a (**3**) bravely / brave lad. Me? What a laugh! My legs were shaking very (**4**) badly / bad. I didn't think I could walk, much less jump! I'm really glad he was with me. We fell for a few minutes, but it seemed like hours! He pulled the cord to open the (**5**) parachute / flippers when it was time. I was really (**6**) amazing / amazed by the view. I've attached a photo of our group to show you. You have to try it sometime!

Bye for now,

Rodney

**E** Read the *Exam Reminder*. Then complete the *Exam Task*.

## Exam Task

Read the sentences about Sophie's scuba diving experience. Choose the best word (**a**, **b** or **c**) for each answer.

1. At first I thought scuba diving was a very _____ thing to try.
   a scared          b scary          c scaring
2. My instructor and I jumped _____ the water together.
   a out of          b onto           c into
3. The diving gear was heavy, so I sank rather _____!
   a quick           b quicker        c quickly
4. My instructor stayed _____ to me, so it was OK.
   a near            b next           c beside
5. He was a _____ teacher and I learnt a lot!
   a good            b best           c well

## Exam Reminder

**Choosing the missing word**
- Read the sentences and see if you can guess what word is missing.
- Then look at the options to see if your guess is there.
- If your guess isn't there, try each option in the gap and think about which one seems correct.

# Grammar

## Present Perfect (1); First Conditional

**A** Choose the correct answers.

1 I've _____ through a rainforest before.
   a walk          b walked

2 We've _____ to 56 different countries.
   a travelled     b travel

3 She's _____ giraffes in Africa.
   a saw           b seen

4 They've _____ from New York to Singapore.
   a flown         b flew

5 Mum isn't here because she's _____ to the chemist's.
   a went          b gone

6 Have you _____ across a lake before?
   a swum          b swam

**B** Circle the correct words.

1 We visited / have visited my aunt's house yesterday.
2 Jan has eaten / ate octopus three times in her life.
3 They closed / have closed the museum at 5 p.m. this afternoon.
4 I have never been / didn't go to Russia before.
5 Have you taken / Did you take lots of photos on your trip so far?
6 Jill didn't talk / hasn't talked to her friend last night.

**C** Complete the sentences with the First Conditional form of the verbs in brackets.

1 If we get up early, we _____ (go) for a hike up the mountain.
2 I _____ (ask) Georgina about bungee jumping if I see her today.
3 If they _____ (pay) extra, the captain will take them further out to sea.
4 We'll try a different route if this one _____ (be) too difficult.
5 If you _____ (not buy) your tickets in advance, you'll have to wait in a long queue.

**D** Complete the dialogues with the Present Perfect form of *be* or *go*.

1 **A:** Where's Kyle and Mark?
   **B:** They _____ to the library.

2 **A:** What's Paris like?
   **B:** I don't know. I _____ there.

3 **A:** Can I speak to Michelle?
   **B:** She _____ out. She'll be back soon.

4 **A:** What do you think of the new stadium?
   **B:** I love it! I _____ twice already.

**E** Read the *Exam Reminder*. Then complete the *Exam Task*.

## Exam Reminder

**Checking for the parts of a tense**
- Identify tenses by looking at the whole sentence around the gap.
- Look for parts that identify the tense and if it needs words like *do*, *will* or *have*.
- Check for negatives or questions as these can affect verb agreements.

## Exam Task

Read the story about Dave's cousin. Choose the best word (**a**, **b** or **c**) for each space.

### My adventurous cousin

Everyone (1) _____ of skiing before. It's a very difficult sport. I (2) _____ it once while on holiday. I didn't enjoy it much and, as with any sport, if you don't like it, you (3) _____ good at it. My cousin, on the other hand, loves it. He has (4) _____ to the ski slopes hundreds of times in his life. In fact, he does more than the usual trip nowadays. A year ago, he (5) _____ to Greenland to go heli-skiing. This is when you jump out of a helicopter to go skiing. If you (6) _____ what you're doing, you will definitely get hurt! He (7) _____ from a helicopter about four times already, and he says each time is better than the last. I (8) _____ him in a video last night and, to be honest, that's exciting enough for me!

1  a hears         b heard        c has heard
2  a have tried    b tried        c will try
3  a are           b will be      c won't be
4  a gone          b been         c done
5  a travels       b has travelled c travelled
6  a don't know    b know         c won't know
7  a will jump     b has jumped   c jumped
8  a watched       b have watched c won't watch

# Listening

**A** Read the *Exam Reminder*. What detailed information will you listen for in each *Exam Task* question?

_____

**B** 🔊 9.1 ▶ Listen and complete the *Exam Task*.

## Exam Reminder

**Focusing on specific information**

- You must listen for detailed information in this type of listening task.
- As you listen, look at the options so you know what to listen for.
- Check answers that you are not sure about when you listen the second time.

## Exam Task

Listen to Deidre and her friend Stan talking about bungee jumping.
For each question, choose the right answer (**a**, **b** or **c**). You will hear the conversation twice.

**1** Where does the bungee jumping take place?
- **a** a car park
- **b** a high bridge
- **c** a tall building

**2** How high is the bungee jump?
- **a** 75 metres
- **b** 85 metres
- **c** 95 metres

**3** At what age can you do it?
- **a** 13 and up
- **b** 14 and up
- **c** 15 and up

**4** When does Deidre want to go?
- **a** Friday    **b** Saturday    **c** Sunday

**5** How much will they pay when they go?
- **a** £34    **b** £38    **c** £48

**C** 🔊 9.2 ▶ Listen again and check your answers.

# Writing: a blog

**A** Complete the blog using the correct adjectival forms of the words in brackets.

## Learning Reminder

**Thinking about your readers**

- A blog is like a diary that you want everyone to see. You show readers your personality and what matters to you the most.
- Blogs often have pictures and links to websites, and sometimes they ask readers to take some action.
- Blogs usually have short paragraphs with headings and subheadings.
- Readers often make comments and it's important to write back.

○ ○ ○   My canyon adventure

https://www.adventureblogs.org.uk

### *My canyon adventure!*

Guys, you'll be (1) _____ (amaze) by what I did this summer. My best friend Robbie and I went mountain biking at the Grand Canyon! It was a (2) _____ (thrill) adventure.

### *South Rim bike path*
There are two trails – the North Rim and the South Rim. We took the South Rim and the map of it is at www.mygc.com/southrim. It seemed like the less (3) _____ (tire) trail. We travelled along Hermit Road. It's about 16 kilometres and we were (4) _____ (exhaust) after we finished!

### *A biker-friendly place*
The location is very nice for bikers. I was (5) _____ (surprise) to learn that there was a bus that takes you and your bike back to the starting point. The paths were in good condition and were also well-marked. It was not a (6) _____ (disappoint) trip in the least!

### *Live your dream*
I urge everyone to experience such a great adventure. It was worth spending the money to get there and the memories will last a lifetime!

**B** Read the blog in A again and answer the questions.

1 What is the main heading?

_____

2 What are the subheadings?

_____

_____

_____

3 How many paragraphs are in the blog?

_____

4 What link did the writer include?

_____

5 What call to action does the reader mention?

_____

**C** Read the email and advert and correct the mistakes in the student's certificate.

> Look back at both texts to check your information after you've completed the notes.

**Email Message**

To whom it may concern,

Some things were wrong on my certificate. I completed the course on the 12th of August. It was the full-day course, not the half-day one. Can you print another one for me?

Thanks,
John Meyers

**Ashton Windsurfing Club**

Courses in windsurfing

Beginner's course (half-day) — four hours, Joy Marina

Intermediate course (full-day) — eight hours, Ford Island

**Ashton Windsurfing Club**

certifies that _____Jonathan Myers_____ completed four hours of training for our _____Beginner's_____ course on the _____11th of August_____ at our Joy Marina location.

> Check for spelling mistakes that we can make when we're in a hurry.

1 _____

2 _____

3 _____

4 _____

5 _____

**D** Read and complete the *Exam Task*. Don't forget to use the *Useful Expressions* on page 119 of your Student's Book.

## Exam Task

Read the news advert and the blog. Fill in the information in the contestant's entry form.

**5th annual Leicester Martial Arts Competition**

at Discovery Stadium

Dates:  karate and kickboxing – 23rd October
         taekwondo and judo – 24th October

Events start at 2 p.m.

**Leicester Martial Arts Competition**

Name:        (1) _____
Sport:       (2) _____
Event date:  (3) _____
Location:    (4) _____
Team name:   (5) _____

**Ryan Marshall's blog        13th Oct**

### Taekwondo event!

Listen, everyone! My martial arts competition is in a week and a half. Don't miss it! Come and cheer for my team, the Wollaton Taekwondo Club!

Leave a comment to say you'll be there, or email me at highkick@email.com for more information. Looking forward to it!

⟳ Writing Reference p. 177 in Student's Book

# Reading

**A** Read the *Exam Reminder*. Where can you see the signs in the *Exam Task*?

_____

**B** Now complete the *Exam Task*.

## Exam Reminder

**Finding words with similar meanings**

- The signs in this task appear in places you know. Think about where you can see them.
- The notices and the descriptions have got words with similar meanings. Underline or circle those words to help you answer the questions.

## Exam Task

Which notice (**A – H**) says this (**1 – 5**)?

1 This costs less than £2. ☐
2 It's fine to drink this. ☐
3 You cannot throw things away here. ☐
4 Your car goes behind the building. ☐
5 You have to pay somewhere else. ☐

A

B

C

D

E

F

G

H

# Vocabulary

**A** Unjumble the fruit and vegetables.

1 ototap      _____
2 torarc      _____
3 lpeaneipp      _____
4 matoto      _____
5 gerona      _____
6 weyratsrbr      _____
7 odacavo      _____
8 urifcawolle      _____
9 iberagenu      _____
10 enegr eabn      _____
11 malerowten      _____
12 nolem      _____
13 ananba      _____
14 aperg      _____

**B** Choose the correct answers.

| bread cheese eggs milk rice yoghurt |

1 I pour _____ in my cereal and have it for breakfast.
2 Would you like some jam to go on your slice of _____?
3 Pasta is delicious when you put grated _____ on top of it.
4 For supper, we're having vegetables with brown _____.
5 I like to mix fresh fruit with _____ to have a nice, healthy dessert.
6 How can anyone eat raw _____? They have to be cooked!

**C** Choose the correct answers.

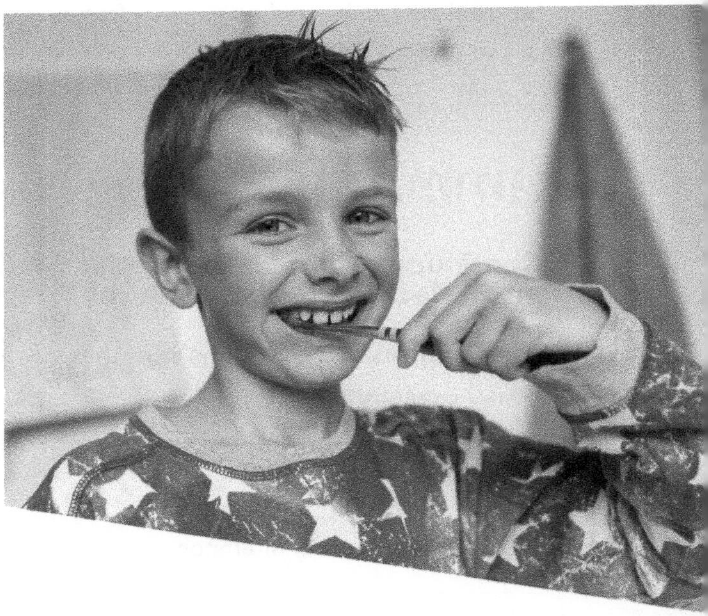

1 My parents tell me to _____ my teeth twice a day.
   a do      b wash      c brush
2 I _____ the doctor for my yearly check-up.
   a went      b stayed      c visited
3 Foods with _____ are very good for your bones.
   a healthy      b protein      c calcium
4 My mum _____ my temperature because I felt warm.
   a did      b took      c felt
5 When I want something sweet, I often eat _____.
   a crisps      b vitamins      c biscuits
6 I was out in the rain yesterday and I think I _____ a cold.
   a got      b took      c ache

**D** Match the words to make collocations.

1 a broken ☐      a decay
2 stomach ☐      b ache
3 tooth ☐      c medicine
4 green ☐      d arm
5 take ☐      e temperature
6 high ☐      f beans

**E** **Choose the correct answers.**

New year, new diet!

https://www.new_year.org/blog/2nd january

**New year, new diet!**
2nd Jan

Since it's a new year, my friend Josh and I decided to start eating healthily! The first thing on the list is no more (1) _____ drinks. They're so bad for you! They're full of (2) _____ and it's much better to drink water when you're (3) _____. Secondly, we're going to eat more (4) _____ fruit and vegetables. They're delicious and full of (5) _____. Last, we're going to say no to (6) _____ food from now on. It may be cheap and easy, but it's the worst thing to put in your body. Wish us luck!

| 1 | **a** salty | **b** fizzy | **c** fried |
|---|---|---|---|
| 2 | **a** sugar | **b** bread | **c** fat |
| 3 | **a** hungry | **b** tired | **c** thirsty |
| 4 | **a** cooked | **b** fresh | **c** frozen |
| 5 | **a** vitamins | **b** meat | **c** protein |
| 6 | **a** raw | **b** fizzy | **c** unhealthy |

# Grammar

## Past Continuous; *Should*, Imperatives & Other expressions; Present Perfect (2); Reflexive Verbs

**A** **Write sentences and questions with these words and the Past Continuous.**

1 Beth / study / all night

_____

2 I / chop / vegetables / half an hour

_____

3 we / swim / yesterday afternoon

_____

4 I / tidy / my room / this morning

_____

5 you / jog / at 8 a.m. / ?

_____

6 they / not lie / in bed / all day

_____

**B** Complete the sentences with the Past Continuous or the Past Simple of the verbs in brackets.

1 Jill _____ (**take**) her friend's photo when she slipped and fell over.
2 It _____ (**snow**) the morning Karen left for her big exam.
3 I _____ (**be**) cold so I put on my coat.
4 The sun was shining, the birds were singing and the kids _____ (**run**) round the garden.
5 Nancy was feeling very tired when she _____ (**get**) home from work.
6 Jessica was calling her friend when she _____ (**drop**) her phone.

**C** Tick (✓) the sentence that's correct.

1 A I've just eaten a whole sandwich. ☐
  B I just have eaten a whole sandwich. ☐
2 A They haven't arrived yet home. ☐
  B They haven't arrived home yet. ☐
3 A We've seen that film already. ☐
  B We've seen already that film. ☐
4 A They haven't sent the invitations yet. ☐
  B They haven't sent the invitations already. ☐
5 A Helen's called in sick to work just. ☐
  B Helen's just called in sick to work. ☐
6 A Have you just finished your assignment? ☐
  B Already have you finished your assignment? ☐

**D** Circle the correct words.

**Scott:** I want to get fit and eat healthier. Have you got any ideas?
**Margie:** (1) Shouldn't you / Why don't you look for a good diet online?
**Scott:** I was thinking about doing that, but I don't know where to look.
**Margie:** You (2) find / should find a good website from a health service or a food specialist.
**Scott:** Yes, but there are so many different sites. It's too much work.
**Margie:** (3) Don't / Why don't you let that stop you. I'm sure one of them has got a great diet if you take the time to look.
**Scott:** Well, it's hard to eat healthily because I really love fast food!
**Margie:** Hmm. You (4) don't / shouldn't eat that sort of food. It's very bad for you!
**Scott:** Well, I need to do something soon. I can't go on like this!
**Margie:** (5) Look / Should look for a diet now. I can help you if you like!

**E** Complete the sentences with reflexive pronouns.

1 We made these gingerbread biscuits _____.
2 I burnt _____ on the oven this morning!
3 She spilt coffee on _____ as she was leaving the house.
4 He took a good look at _____ in the mirror.
5 The students can find the answers _____ without my help.
6 Don't cut _____ on that sharp knife!
7 We don't bathe a cat. A cat can clean _____.
8 Kyle and Tom, keep _____ busy while I go out.

# Listening

**A** Read the *Exam Reminder*. What differences do you see in the pictures of each *Exam Task* question?

_____

**B** 10.1 ▶️ Listen and complete the *Exam Task*.

## Exam Task

You will hear five short conversations. You will hear each conversation twice. There is one question for each conversation. For each question, choose the right answer (**a**, **b** or **c**).

**1** What is Nicholas putting in the salad?

   a            b             c

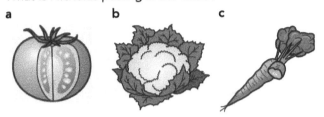

**2** What part of Jane's body hurts?

   a            b             c

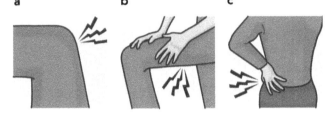

**3** At what time is Beth's family eating?

   a            b             c

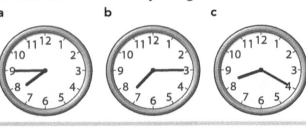

**4** Where does Sam go jogging?

   a            b             c

**5** How many people turned up for the race?

   a            b             c

**C** 10.2 ▶️ Listen again and check your answers.

# Writing: a note

**A** Complete the sentences with one word in each gap.

1 Hey Tom. _____, but I can't come to your football match.

2 Dear Ms Tomsen, I _____ that I could not visit your office.

3 Sorry, Jill, but I'm _____ I've got some other things to deal with.

4 I wasn't at the performance _____ there was a traffic accident.

5 Dear Mr Jones, I _____ attend today's meeting due to illness.

6 I'm sorry I missed your wedding, _____ I promise to make it up to you.

> **Apologising & making excuses**
> - We say we are sorry about something when we apologise. We usually give a reason to say why.
> - There are different ways to apologise. In formal writing, we can say *I apologise* and in informal writing, we can say *I'm sorry*.
> - To give the reason, we can start with *I am afraid that* ... in formal writing and *I'm afraid that* ... in informal writing.
> - Learn the different ways of apologising and giving excuses using both formal and informal language.

**B** In Column 1, write 'A' for apologies and 'B' for excuses. In Column 2, write 'A' for formal and 'B' for informal.

|  | Column 1 | Column 2 |
|---|---|---|
| 1 Hey Jack, really sorry I missed your birthday party. | ☐ | ☐ |
| 2 Hi Jan, I'm afraid I have another event to go to. | ☐ | ☐ |
| 3 I missed the concert yesterday because I was not well. | ☐ | ☐ |
| 4 Dear Ms Wu, I apologise that I could not attend the opening. | ☐ | ☐ |
| 5 I've got another appointment today, so let's meet tomorrow. | ☐ | ☐ |
| 6 My apologies, but I could not be at the presentation. | ☐ | ☐ |

**C** Write sentences that you can use in a reply to the messages with the words below. Use formal or informal language.

> Reasons and excuses can help expand answers.

> Ensure you know what words come after the expressions you use.

Hank and I are cooking some burgers on the barbecue. Do you want to come over later for lunch in the garden?

● ● ○ ○ Email Message

The restaurant is celebrating its one-year anniversary. As a valued customer, we'd like to invite you to the celebration. Please confirm if you will be attending.

> Check you know what the situation is and if you need to use formal or informal language.

1 sorry / not make it / lunch

_____

2 have got a lot of work / this afternoon

_____

3 thanks / ask / have fun

_____

4 many thanks / your invitation / one-year anniversary

_____

5 unfortunately / not able / attend

_____

6 accept / apologies / hope / return to restaurant soon

_____

**D** Read and complete the *Exam Task*. Don't forget to use the *Useful Expressions* on page 131 of your Student's Book.

## Exam Task

Read the text message from Keira.

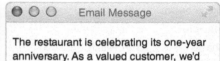

Hi Amy, I was hoping to see you at the party. Why didn't you come? You said you were bringing a cake. It's OK because there was plenty of food. Did you see the text I sent you that night? I didn't get a reply. I'm a bit worried about you. Are we still meeting today?

Write a text message to Keira and answer the questions. Write **25–35** words.

# Vocabulary

**A** Choose the correct answers.

1 The kids jumped _____ the big swimming pool.
   a into          c under
   b over          d off

2 You need a good _____ for skydiving!
   a ice axe       c parachute
   b wetsuit       d board

3 After a long day of playing sport, Julie was _____.
   a interesting   c tiring
   b interested    d tired

4 I like how Jake swims. He's a very _____ swimmer.
   a bad           c well
   b badly         d good

5 She put lots of _____ in the salad.
   a biscuits      c milk
   b carrots       d doughnuts

6 I want something salty. I think I'll have some _____.
   a tomatoes      c watermelon
   b biscuits      d crisps

7 I think _____ looks funny. It's big and white, and it looks like a head!
   a pineapple     c cauliflower
   b avocado       d bread

8 We can't eat this food because it's _____.
   a cooked        c fresh
   b frozen        d healthy

9 I'm going to the dentist. I've got a _____.
   a toothache     c headache
   b stomach ache  d temperature

10 Make sure you _____ your teeth before you go to bed.
   a do            c wash
   b make          d brush

11 Don't jump _____ the bridge. You'll get hurt!
   a onto          c off
   b into          d over

12 The cat was in the tree, but then it jumped _____.
   a onto          c into
   b over          d down

13 The film is very _____. I can't watch!
   a exhausted     c frightened
   b exhausting    d frightening

14 You're going to need knee pads for _____.
   a surfing       c scuba diving
   b skateboarding d skiing

15 Put this _____ on your head so you don't hurt it.
   a mask          c stick
   b crampon       d helmet

16 These _____ are not clean. I can't see anything!
   a elbow pads    c flippers
   b goggles       d skis

17 I don't drink _____ drinks because they've got a lot of sugar.
   a raw           c fizzy
   b delicious     d juicy

18 The mountain was high, but Lance climbed it _____.
   a brave         c dangerously
   b bravely       d dangerous

19 She wasn't feeling well so she _____ in bed.
   a did           c stayed
   b hurt          d took

20 I'm quite _____. I'll get some water.
   a hungry        c healthy
   b tired         d thirsty

# Grammar

**B** **Choose the correct answers.**

1 Have you had anything to eat yet?'
'No, _____.'
- **a** I haven't
- **c** I did
- **b** I have
- **d** I didn't

2 Michelle has _____ a marathon race.
- **a** runs
- **c** run
- **b** running
- **d** ran

3 'Where is David?'
'He's _____ to the shops.'
- **a** be
- **c** been
- **b** went
- **d** gone

4 '_____ in an aeroplane before?'
'Yes, I have.'
- **a** Are you flying
- **c** Have you flown
- **b** You have flown
- **d** Did you fly

5 If I have the money, I _____ to Thailand this autumn.
- **a** have travelled
- **c** travel
- **b** am travelling
- **d** will travel

6 'I don't want to study for my exam.'
'You won't pass if you _____!'
- **a** studied
- **c** won't study
- **b** study
- **d** don't study

7 If you pay for _____ buy tomorrow's lunch.
- **a** dinner I
- **c** dinner, I'll
- **b** dinner. I'll
- **d** dinner I'll

8 'How was the weather yesterday?'
'It was raining and the wind _____.'
- **a** blew
- **c** blows
- **b** was blowing
- **d** is blowing

9 Tom was jogging in the park when he _____ a tree.
- **a** was hitting
- **c** hits
- **b** hit
- **d** is hitting

10 'I'm really tired.'
'You _____ get some rest.'
- **a** should
- **c** don't
- **b** shouldn't
- **d** don't you

11 'Are you at home now?'
'Yes, _____ back from the cleaners.'
- **a** I just come
- **c** I've just come
- **b** just I've come
- **d** I've come just

12 Niles _____ visited the Great Wall of China.
- **a** has
- **c** is
- **b** have
- **d** does

13 'Why are you going to hospital?'
'I've _____ my leg.'
- **a** broke
- **c** break
- **b** breaks
- **d** broken

14 'Are you feeling better now?'
'Yes. I _____ a really bad headache.'
- **a** 'm having
- **c** was having
- **b** had
- **d** have

15 Sean took a photo of _____ with his smartphone.
- **a** yourself
- **c** itself
- **b** himself
- **d** ourselves

16 'We went to Bruges last spring.'
'Oh, I've _____ there before.'
- **a** been ever
- **c** ever been
- **b** been never
- **d** never been

17 Jill _____ the rubbish out last night at midnight.
- **a** is taking
- **c** has taken
- **b** took
- **d** takes

18 'What happened to Jane and Doug?'
'They hurt _____ moving a sofa.'
- **a** themselves
- **c** himself
- **b** yourselves
- **d** herself

19 Laura hasn't finished her art project _____.
- **a** ever
- **c** yet
- **b** just
- **d** already

20 'I'd like to learn French.'
'_____ take some lessons?'
- **a** Shouldn't you
- **c** You don't
- **b** Should you
- **d** Why don't you

# 11 Be Creative!

## Reading

**A** Read the *Exam Reminder*. Which responses in the *Exam Task* are for *Yes / No* questions?

_____

**B** Now complete the *Exam Task*.

### Exam Reminder

**Identifying the type of question**

- Look for *Wh-* questions and *Yes / No* questions in the dialogue. You can underline *Wh-* questions and star (*) *Yes / No* questions to help you.
- Look for answers that go with these types of questions. If a response begins with *Yes* or *No*, it will not go with a *Wh-* question.

## Exam Task

Complete the dialogue between two friends. What does Henry tell Alice?
Choose the correct answer **A – H**. There are three letters you do not need to use.

**Alice:** Have you ever made a film using your smartphone?
**Henry:** (1) _____
**Alice:** What have you filmed before?
**Henry:** (2) _____
**Alice:** Did it turn out well?
**Henry:** (3) _____
**Alice:** How did you do that?
**Henry:** (4) _____
**Alice:** Can you show me how to use it?
**Henry:** (5) _____
**Alice:** Great! I want to make my own film!

**A** I used a program for filmmaking. It's great fun, actually.
**B** Yes, I've made one or two films for fun.
**C** I made the film a few days ago.
**D** No, I used my computer to make the film.
**E** Of course! I'd love to do that.
**F** I filmed my family's beach holiday last year.
**G** No, I've never been in a film before.
**H** Yes, it did. I used my computer to make changes.

# Vocabulary

**A** Match these words to the photos.

audience   author   conductor   musician   orchestra   stage

1 _____

2 _____

3 _____

4 _____

5 _____

6 _____

**B** Complete the sentences with the correct form of these words.

angry   happy   loud   quick   quiet   slow

1 Hurry up and take these photos _____ so we can go home!
2 Please speak _____ so I can understand you.
3 The main characters fell in love and the story ended _____.
4 They spoke _____ so no one was able to hear them.
5 The audience clapped _____ at the end of the great performance.
6 The teacher spoke _____ because the students were upsetting her.

**C** Circle the correct words.

1 She was bad at / of singing, so she decided to learn an instrument instead.
2 I'm interested in / to taking a class in performance art.
3 The conductor was happy about / for getting a good review.
4 She's not keen on / to acting for a live audience.
5 Julie was famous in / for her amazing paintings of elephants.
6 I'm tired of / about always watching films from the 90s.

**D** Match the words to the definitions.

1 Books often have interesting artwork on this. ☐      **a** title
2 This is the name of a book, film or theatrical production. ☐      **b** back cover
3 There is a bit of information about the story on this. ☐      **c** canvas
4 This is a passage between rows of seats in a theatre. ☐      **d** villain
5 This is a bad character in a story. ☐      **e** aisle
6 This is a strong cloth that artists paint on. ☐      **f** front cover

**E** Read the *Exam Reminder*. Then complete the *Exam Task*.

### Exam Task

Read the sentences about Joan's dance class.
Choose the best word (**a**, **b** or **c**) for each answer.

1 I'm taking a dance class because it's very _____.
   **a** energy     **b** energetic     **c** energetically

2 I love my teacher because she dances so _____.
   **a** beautiful     **b** beauty     **c** beautifully

3 She's famous _____ dancing in Broadway musicals.
   **a** for     **b** in     **c** on

4 I was quite bad _____ dancing in the beginning, but my teacher's helping a lot.
   **a** with     **b** about     **c** at

5 I would like to dance on _____ one day, if I'm good enough!
   **a** aisle        **b** row        **c** stage

### Exam Reminder

**Choosing the correct option**
- Some options may seem obvious, but for others you may not be certain.
- When you are not sure, try each option and choose the word that 'feels' best. Read the sentence to yourself and check that your choice makes sense.

# Grammar

## The Passive Voice: Present Simple; The Passive Voice: Past Simple; Narrative Tenses

**A** Write sentences with these words and the passive of the Present Simple.

1 pencils / make / wood and carbon
_____

2 the letter / print / fine paper
_____

3 whales / see / the Pacific Ocean
_____

4 this song / sing / during the holidays
_____

5 most homes / build / by hand
_____

6 the site / photograph / by famous photographers
_____

**B** Rewrite the sentences in the passive of the Past Simple.

1 A computer built this home.

_____

2 Picasso drew these drawings.

_____

3 Charles Dickens wrote this famous story.

_____

4 They opened Disney World in 1971.

_____

5 They made the sculptures from ice.

_____

6 The author signed the books.

_____

**C** Complete the sentences with the Past Continuous or the Past Simple form of the verbs in brackets.

1 Max was playing in his living room when his parents _____ (**tell**) him to go to bed.
2 While Max _____ (**walk**) to his room, he made a special wish.
3 When he woke up the next morning, he _____ (**live**) on an island with lots of animals!
4 The animals were running around when Max _____ (**arrive**).
5 As Max _____ (**play**) with the animals, he thought about his worried parents.
6 In the end, Max got lonely and _____ (**return**) to his home.

**D** Put the sentences of the story in the correct order.

a While sitting on the sofa, Oscar the cat asked Lenny and Josie to play games with him.  ☐

b Lenny and Josie were tidying the house while the cat was making more of a mess.  ☐

c While the three of them were playing, they made a huge mess in the house.  ☐

d In the end, the cat ran out of the house and took all the mess with him!  ☐

e Lenny and Josie were studying when there was a knock on the front door.  ☐

f When they opened the door, a cat named Oscar came inside and sat on their sofa.  ☐

**E** Read the *Exam Reminder*. Then complete the *Exam Task*.

## Exam Reminder

**Reading the whole text**
- Read the whole text to get the general idea. Then read each sentence, one at a time. For each gap, identify the kind of word you need.
- With your answers in place, read through the whole text again to check that it makes sense. Also check your spelling.

## Exam Task

Read a student's text about their favourite author. Write **ONE** word for each space.

### J.K. Rowling

J.K. Rowling is one of my favourite authors. The *Harry Potter* books (**1**) _____ written by her. She wrote the first book, *Harry Potter and the Philosopher's Stone*, (**2**) _____1997. She went on to write six more Harry Potter books between 1998 and 2005. Each book (**3**) _____ eventually made into a great film. The story follows Harry Potter, a boy with magical powers. He finds out about his powers while he (**4**) _____ living with his aunt and uncle. He leaves to go to a school for wizards, known (**5**) _____ Hogwarts School of Witchcraft and Wizardry, at Hogwarts Castle. There, he meets amazing characters (**6**) _____ finds himself in great danger. Rowling (**7**) _____ written other books about Harry's world and I really enjoy (**8**) _____ them!

# Listening

**A** Read the *Exam Reminder*. In which gaps in the *Exam Task* questions will you write times or dates?

_____

**Exam Reminder**

**Listening for times & dates**

- To become more familiar with times and dates, practise saying them and talking about them.
- The *Exam Task* often needs times and dates. Look for the gaps that need them before you start.

**B** ▐11.1▐▬▌ Listen and complete the *Exam Task*.

## Exam Task

You will hear a radio presenter talking about an orchestra. Listen and complete each question. You will hear the information twice.

**Superhero Orchestra**

| | |
|---|---|
| Number of members: | **(1)** _____ |
| In town: | from the **(2)** _____ to the 30th of June |
| Date of prize performance: | **(3)** _____ |
| Start time: | **(4)** _____ |
| Address: | **(5)** _____ Shelton Lane |

**C** ▐11.2▐▬▌ Listen again and check your answers.

# Writing: a short narrative

**A** Complete the story with these words.

| after   as soon as   at first   before   eventually   suddenly |
|---|

Hank was getting ready for school one morning.
**(1)** _____, everything seemed fine. He made some toast for breakfast and sat down at the table.
**(2)** _____, his dog Lucy walked past him – she was carrying the laundry and walking on two legs!
**(3)** _____ Hank saw this, he dropped his toast. Hank was shocked, but **(4)** _____, he got up and followed Lucy to the washing machine.
**(5)** _____ he was able to say a word, Lucy turned around and said, 'Oh … Hello, Hank.'

Hank slowly replied, 'Hhhhello?'

Lucy opened the washing machine door and **(6)** _____ she put the laundry and the washing powder in it she closed the door and started it. She then said, 'I know … I can talk, can't I? I don't understand it! And I really don't understand how Jude the cat is making calls on your smartphone.'

**Learning Reminder**

**Using a writing formula**

- Narratives describe experiences and events. Use a formula to help you organise this type of writing.
- Divide your story into three paragraphs. The beginning paragraph sets the scene: it's the *who*, *when* and *where* of your story. The middle paragraph says what happened or what the problem is. The final paragraph gives a solution and a conclusion.
- Use connecting words in your writing to make it more interesting and easier to follow.

**B** **Choose the correct draft of the next part of the story in A.**

The news was showing reports of cats and dogs walking and talking all around the globe. They were doing all sorts of things. They were running businesses and flying aeroplanes. They were even giving news reports! But some pets were not as good as Lucy and Jude. They wanted to put humans in zoos. Lucy, Jude and the good pets of the world were not going to let that happen.

**1** ☐
– cats and dogs walk and talk
– cats start running businesses
– cats put dogs to work
– dogs start fighting cats

**2** ☐
– pets giving the news
– people and pets working together
– pets take control of everything
– Lucy and Jude join them

**3** ☐
– news reports about pets
– pets doing things people do
– bad pets harming people
– Lucy and Jude protecting people

**C** **Tick (✓) the sentences that will appear in the final paragraph of the story in A according to the writer's draft.**

Make a habit of writing first drafts.

– final plan ... a chess match
– losers must leave forever
– Jude for good team, Jacob (bear) for bad
– Jacob, big paws, couldn't play
– Jude played like a champion
– Jude wins, bad pets leave forever

Review your draft and think of ways to improve it.

Review your work and check for correct spelling, punctuation and grammar.

1  Lucy and Jude put their final plan in place – a chess match between the best of the good pets and the best of the bad ones. ☐
2  They agreed that the loser's team had to leave the planet and never come back. ☐
3  The good team chose Jude to play for them and the bad team chose Jacob the bear. ☐
4  At first, Lucy thought Jude was a bad choice. He was a cat, after all. 'How smart can he be?' thought Lucy. ☐
5  Jacob couldn't move the pieces with his big paws and Jude played very well. ☐
6  In the end, Jude cleverly won the match and the bad pets had to go far, far away, never to be seen again. ☐

**D** **Read and complete the *Exam Task*. Don't forget to use the *Useful Expressions* on page 145 of your Student's Book.**

Exam Task

Read the advert for a writing competition and the student's email. Complete the contest entry form.

**Young Reader's Digest** is accepting entries for the 'Spring Writing Competition'.

For this month's contest, we're looking for works of fiction.

Your stories should be no more than 1,000 words.

The winner will see their story in our June issue.

Visit www.yrd.com/springcontest for more information.

---

● ○ ○       Email Message

To: Dana Pratts
From: Tony Sims <tsims@fastmail.com>
Re: Writing competition

Hi Dana,
I wanted to share my idea for the creative writing competition. I'm writing a story about our neighbourhood pets. I'm calling it 'Planet of the Pets'. It's a funny title, isn't it? I'll send the first draft as soon as I've written it.
Talk soon,
Tony

---

**Young Reader's Digest**

| | | | |
|---|---|---|---|
| Student's name: | (1) _____ | Type of work: | (4) _____ |
| Name of contest: | (2) _____ | Contact information: | (5) _____ |
| Title of entry: | (3) '_____' | | |

▶ Writing Reference p. 180 in Student's Book

# Reading

**A** Read the *Exam Reminder*. What can you give as a response that's not a simple *no*?

_____

**B** Now complete the *Exam Task*.

## Exam Task

Complete the five conversations. Choose **a**, **b** or **c**.

**1** Shall we book a flight to Hawaii?
  **a** Yes, let's stay there.
  **b** Good idea!
  **c** I'm going by car.

**2** What do you think of Jamaica?
  **a** That's great!
  **b** I've only been once.
  **c** It sounds interesting.

**3** I've forgotten my passport.
  **a** You can buy one there.
  **b** It's OK. I've got mine.
  **c** Oh, no! That's terrible.

**4** Why don't we go to the park today?
  **a** They don't want to.
  **b** Sorry, I'm busy at the moment.
  **c** I don't like the beach.

**5** Shall we go by bus or by train?
  **a** Yes, good idea!
  **b** Let's do both.
  **c** Either is fine.

# Vocabulary

## A Circle the correct words.

1 The plane is boarding / landing now. Please have your tickets ready.
2 Madam, you have to check / place in your suitcase.
3 After you leave the plane, you wait / go through passport control.
4 When you're in a car, you have to wear / serve a seatbelt.
5 I can help you find / reserve your seat on board.
6 We had to wait / work in the airport for three hours!

## B Match the words to make collocations.

| 1 | security | ☐ | a | map |
|---|----------|----|----|----------|
| 2 | outdoor | ☐ | b | ship |
| 3 | weather | ☐ | c | control |
| 4 | departure | ☐ | d | activity |
| 5 | cruise | ☐ | e | cream |
| 6 | sun | ☐ | f | area |

## C Match these weather words to the photos.

cloudy   cold   rainy   snowy   stormy   sunny

1 _____

2 _____

3 _____

4 _____

5 _____

6 _____

**D** Choose the correct answers.

1 You have to have your _____ with you to travel to another country.

   **a** suitcase            **b** passport

2 Let's take the _____. It's a lot faster than driving on the smaller roads.

   **a** motorway         **b** platform

3 We're taking a long trip on the ferry, so we're sleeping in a _____.

   **a** journey           **b** cabin

4 Did you buy any _____ to remember your trip?

   **a** photos            **b** souvenirs

5 We took a _____ to the airport early in the morning.

   **a** plane             **b** taxi

6 Are they serving any _____ on this flight?

   **a** food              **b** seats

**E** Complete the text conversation with prepositions.

**12.14 P.M.**   Hey Jordan. We're sitting (**1**) _____ the beach right now. Do you want to come and join us?

**12.17 P.M.**   I can't. I'm going for a walk (**2**) _____ the forest with Jake.

**12.20 P.M.**   Oh, that sounds boring! You're (**3**) _____ holiday. The beach is more fun.

**12.21 P.M.**   Well, there's a lot to do here. Tomorrow we're going for a drive (**4**) _____ the mountains. Come and join us for that.

**12.24 P.M.**   Yes. Well, I know a place (**5**) _____ the river that's got great food. We can eat there for a late lunch.

**12.25 P.M.**   Perfect! So, I'll see you (**6**) _____ the hotel later …

**12.26 P.M.**   See you!

# Grammar

## Present Continuous: Future Plans & Arrangements; *Be going to*

**A** Complete the email with the Present Continuous form of the verbs in brackets.

---

000                        Email Message

To: Peter
From: Darren
RE: Weekend travel plans

Hey Peter,
I wanted to send a quick email about this weekend's plans. We **(1)** _____ **(meet)**
John and Marcy at the Hotel Versailles at 2 p.m. From there, we **(2)** _____ **(get)**
on a bus to Lyons. The bus **(3)** _____ **(arrive)** at 8 p.m. My parents are already
there and we **(4)** _____ **(have)** dinner with them around nine. I imagine we'll
be hungry!
On Sunday, my parents and I **(5)** _____ **(drive)** to their cottage in the country.
What **(6)** _____ **(you / do)** that day? You're welcome to come with us.
Bye for now,
Darren

---

**B** Use the ticket to complete the sentences using the Present Continuous form of these verbs.

> board   close   depart   fly   land   sit

1 John Doe _____ from Moscow
   to Larnaka.
2 His flight _____ from Gate 47.
3 He _____ his flight at 11.30.
4 The gate _____ 40 minutes before
   departure.
5 He _____ in seat 24A.
6 His plane _____ in Larnaka in the
   afternoon.

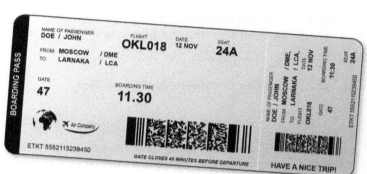

**C** Complete the dialogue with *be going to* and the verbs in brackets.

**Ben:** Have you got plans for the summer, Sarah?

**Sarah:** Yes, I have. I **(1)** _____ **(stay)** with relatives in Jersey.

**Ben:** Ah, I see. How are you getting there?

**Sarah:** I **(2)** _____ **(take)** a train from my house to Poole and then I
**(3)** _____ **(travel)** by ferry to the island.

**Ben:** That sounds like a nice adventure. Are there also planes to the island?

**Sarah:** Yes. I usually go by plane, but I **(4)** _____ **(not fly)** this time.

**Ben:** I hear it can get quite windy in the channel, even in the summer. You **(5)** _____ **(need)**
a good jacket.

**Sarah:** Don't worry, I **(6)** _____ **(pack)** one!

**D** Complete the questions. Use the information in the responses.

1 **A:** Who _____?
   **B:** I'm going to travel with my sister.
2 **A:** When _____?
   **B:** We're going to leave on the 5th of May.
3 **A:** How _____?
   **B:** We're going to get to Amsterdam by plane.

4 **A:** How long _____?
   **B:** We're going to be there for three days.
5 **A:** Where _____?
   **B:** We're going to stay in the Hotel Holland.
6 **A:** What _____?
   **B:** We're going to explore the city on bikes.

**E** Complete the text with one word in each gap.

Travel › Topics › Countries

### TRAVEL TO INDIA!

Hi guys, I'm really excited about my trip to India. I'm going to **(1)** _____ so much fun! I'm leaving on the 23rd of June from London Heathrow Airport. My plane is taking **(2)** _____ at 6.30 a.m. ... I'm going to **(3)** _____ so tired!! Oh well, I plan to sleep on the plane. I'm going **(4)** _____ travel with my whole family. We're staying at a really nice hotel in Mumbai. What **(5)** _____ we going to do in India? I plan on trying some really amazing food. We're also **(6)** _____ to travel to the countryside. I'd love to see an elephant. I think they have those in India, don't they?! So, see you guys when I get back!!

# Listening

**A** Read the *Exam Reminder*. Should you answer all the questions during the first listening?

_____

**B** 🔊 12.1 Listen and complete the *Exam Task*.

## Exam Reminder

**Reviewing your answers**
- You don't have to be in a hurry to choose answers. If you don't know an answer the first time you listen, leave it and move on to the next question.
- Answers are often easier to hear the second time you listen.

## Exam Task

Listen to Bobby complain to his sister, Maggie, about their holiday.
For each question, choose the right answer (**a**, **b** or **c**). You will hear the conversation twice.

1 What did Bobby forget to bring?
   **a** his laptop
   **b** his music player
   **c** his smartphone

2 What does Maggie say Bobby should do for fun?
   **a** read a book
   **b** take photos
   **c** surf the internet

3 What is Maggie going to do at the shop?
   **a** buy souvenirs
   **b** look at things
   **c** wait outside

4 Who will Bobby ask for money?
   **a** Maggie
   **b** his mum
   **c** his dad

5 How much money is Bobby going to ask for?
   **a** ten euros
   **b** 15 euros
   **c** 20 euros

**C** 🔊 12.2 Listen again and check your answers.

# Writing: an invitation

## Learning Reminder

**Writing & responding to an invitation**

- We often use the Present Continuous for future plans when we're writing invitations.
- Invitations should give information about who it's from, what the occasion is, and when and where the event is.
- We can accept or refuse invitations, and when we refuse, we use polite language. Learn the different ways of accepting and refusing invitations.
- We can also offer to help or ask for permission to do something.

**A** Match the answers to the questions.

1 What type of party are you having? ☐
2 Who is having the party? ☐
3 When is the party happening? ☐
4 Where are you having the party? ☐

a It's my best friend Michelle Radcliff's party.
b It's on Saturday the 4th of June from 1 p.m. to 7 p.m.
c We're having a fancy dress party.
d It's at Michelle's house, in her back garden.

**B** Complete the texts with these words.

| come    could I    join    thanks very much    would like    would love |

Michelle and Janice (1) _____ to invite you to a fancy dress party. (2) _____ along to celebrate the beginning of summer!
Saturday, 4th June – 1–7 p.m. at Michelle's house.
(3) _____ us for the party! Email Michelle at mrad@email.com and let us know.

---

○ ○ ○    Email Message

To: Michelle <mrad@email.com>    From: Darren

Hi Michelle,
(4) _____ for the invitation. I (5) _____ to come to your party! I'll dress up as a pilot – that'll be cool!
(6) _____ bring my little brother, Sam? He'd really enjoy it, too. Looking forward to the party!
Darren

**C** Choose an appropriate response, A or B.

1 We're going on a day trip to the mountains. Would you like to come?
  A Thanks for the invitation. I'm afraid I can't make it.
  B Thank you for your invitation. Unfortunately, I will not be able to attend.

2 I can't decide what to do for my anniversary. What should I do?
  A Why don't you go on a week-long trip to a tropical island?
  B That would be a great idea. I'm sure you'll have lots of fun.

3 We're going to the Alps in a week. Would you like to help us plan our trip?
  A Of course. I could bring my travel books. They have some good ideas.
  B I'm sorry but I'm too busy to go on a trip at the moment.

4 We would like to invite you to the wedding of Paul Jones and Lisa Sims.
  A It's my sister's graduation, so I'm sorry but I can't come.
  B Thank you for thinking of us. We would love to attend.

> Make sure you use the right language for the right situation.

> Identify the language function: making a suggestion, asking for advice, making an offer or an invitation, etc.

## Exam Task

**D** Read and complete the *Exam Task*. Don't forget to use the *Useful Expressions* on page 157 of your Student's Book.

Read the invitation from your friend, Elizabeth.

○ ○ ○    Email Message

Re: Fancy dress party

Hi Donald,
The fancy dress party is happening soon. Are you coming? What are you going to wear? The theme is travel. I'm going to dress up as a flight attendant. I was also thinking of having a contest. What do you think I should do?
Talk to you soon,
Elizabeth

Write an email to Elizabeth and answer the questions.
Write **25–35** words.

▶ Writing Reference p. 178 in Student's Book

# Vocabulary

**A** Choose the correct answers.

1 Excuse me, sir, but you're sitting in my _____.
   - **a** aisle
   - **b** stage
   - **c** seat
   - **d** row

2 The audience clapped _____ for the actor.
   - **a** bravely
   - **b** loudly
   - **c** beautifully
   - **d** carefully

3 Please speak _____ so I can understand you.
   - **a** quickly
   - **b** energetically
   - **c** slowly
   - **d** creatively

4 I'm tired _____ watching these silly TV shows.
   - **a** at
   - **b** on
   - **c** of
   - **d** to

5 They were happy _____ seeing their old friends.
   - **a** about
   - **b** for
   - **c** in
   - **d** with

6 She read the _____ to find out about the book.
   - **a** front cover
   - **b** audience
   - **c** author
   - **d** back cover

7 Your flight isn't leaving for an hour. Please _____ in the departure area.
   - **a** go
   - **b** board
   - **c** check
   - **d** wait

8 Your train is arriving at the _____ on your right.
   - **a** cabin
   - **b** seatbelt
   - **c** platform
   - **d** motorway

9 Let's go camping _____ the lake this weekend.
   - **a** in
   - **b** to
   - **c** on
   - **d** by

10 Remember to bring _____ so you don't get burnt.
   - **a** passports
   - **b** souvenirs
   - **c** ice-cream
   - **d** sun cream

11 We can't go to the beach today. It's too _____.
   - **a** bright
   - **b** rainy
   - **c** hot
   - **d** sunny

12 I want to ski, so I hope the mountain is _____.
   - **a** snowy
   - **b** stormy
   - **c** windy
   - **d** cloudy

13 The actors appeared on the _____ in great costumes.
   - **a** row
   - **b** seat
   - **c** aisle
   - **d** stage

14 The football team played _____ and won the game.
   - **a** slowly
   - **b** sadly
   - **c** interestingly
   - **d** energetically

15 I'm keen _____ trying bungee jumping.
   - **a** to
   - **b** in
   - **c** at
   - **d** on

16 I really liked the story, but I hate that it ended _____.
   - **a** happily
   - **b** slowly
   - **c** bravely
   - **d** sadly

17 The musicians watched the _____ as he moved his arms.
   - **a** conductor
   - **b** orchestra
   - **c** group
   - **d** author

18 Did you _____ a seat for our journey?
   - **a** reserve
   - **b** take
   - **c** travel
   - **d** pay

19 I enjoy _____ outdoor activities on holiday.
   - **a** going
   - **b** doing
   - **c** taking
   - **d** having

20 Our hotel is _____ the coast and the view is amazing!
   - **a** to
   - **b** with
   - **c** in
   - **d** on

# Grammar

**B  Choose the correct answers.**

1  This museum _____ by many people each year.
  a  visits
  b  was visited
  c  is visited
  d  visited

2  Souvenirs _____ along the waterfront.
  a  is sold
  b  are sold
  c  sells
  d  sell

3  'Who took this photo?'
  'It _____ by a famous artist.'
  a  is taken
  b  took
  c  was taken
  d  takes

4  The floor in here is made _____ wood.
  a  for
  b  in
  c  by
  d  out of

5  Those flowers _____ by the neighbours.
  a  is picked
  b  was picked
  c  are picked
  d  were picked

6  'This is a really old house.'
  'Yes, it _____ 1893.'
  a  was built in
  b  is built of
  c  was built from
  d  is built in

7  'What were they doing when Ben arrived?'
  'They _____ behind the furniture.'
  a  hid
  b  are hiding
  c  were hiding
  d  hide

8  'What time is your flight today?'
  'It _____ at 3 p.m.'
  a  left
  b  is leaving
  c  was leaving
  d  leave

9  'Where are you going to stay on holiday?'
  'We're _____ in a seaside resort.'
  a  go to stay
  b  stayed
  c  going to stay
  d  stay

10  'What are you going to do tomorrow?'
  'We're _____ in the mountains.'
  a  go hiking
  b  hike
  c  going hiking
  d  go to go hiking

11  Some paintings in the gallery _____ last night.
  a  steal
  b  were stolen
  c  stole
  d  are stolen

12  As Maria was riding her bike, the wheel _____.
  a  broke
  b  was broke
  c  was breaking
  d  broken

13  'How long are you staying in Mexico?'
  'I _____ on the 4th.'
  a  returning
  b  staying
  c  'm returning
  d  'm staying

14  The oven is too hot and the food _____.
  a  goes to burn
  b  burning
  c  burns
  d  is going to burn

15  Jill stopped at the street corner and _____ her mum.
  a  phones
  b  was phoned
  c  phoned
  d  was phoning

16  'Where are you sitting on the plane?'
  'I'm _____ in first class.'
  a  sitting
  b  sit
  c  going to sit
  d  going to be sitting

17  'Didn't your uncle build your home?'
  'No, it was built _____ my grandparents.'
  a  of
  b  in
  c  with
  d  by

18  'When I went on stage, everyone _____.'
  'They were glad to see you!'
  a  was clapping
  b  were clapping
  c  clapped
  d  claps

19  The art project was made _____ plastic bottles.
  a  in
  b  at
  c  from
  d  by

20  It's cold out. Wear a coat or you _____ sick.
  a  get
  b  go to get
  c  are going to get
  d  are getting